Positive
Classroom
Management

But what is social life if not the solving of social problems, behaving properly and pursuing aims acceptable to all?

Maria Montessori, *The Absorbent Mind*

Positive Classroom Management

A Step-by-Step Guide to Successfully Running the Show Without Destroying Student Dignity

Robert DiGiulio

CORWIN PRESS, INC.
A Sage Publications Company
Thousand Oaks, California

For information address:

Corwin Press, Inc.
A Sage Publications Company
2455 Teller Road
Thousand Oaks, California 91320

SAGE Publications Ltd.
6 Bonhill Street
London EC2A 4PU
United Kingdom

SAGE Publications India Pvt. Ltd.
M-32 Market
Greater Kailash I
New Delhi 110 048 India

Printed in the United States of America

Library of Congress Cataloging-in-Publication Data

DiGiulio, Robert C., 1949-
    Positive classroom management: a step-by-step guide to
successfully running the show without destroying student dignity /
Robert DiGiulio.
        p. cm.
    Includes bibliographical references and index.
    ISBN 0-8039-6288-6 (C: alk. paper). — ISBN 0-8039-6289-4 (P:
alk. paper)
    1. Classroom management—United States. I. Title.
LB3013.D54 1995
371.1'024'0973—dc20   95-18298

This book is printed on acid-free paper.

95 96 97 98 99 10 9 8 7 6 5 4 3 2 1

Corwin Press Project Editor: Susan McElroy
Corwin Press Typesetter: Andrea D. Swanson

Contents

Preface   vii

Acknowledgments   xi

About the Author   xiii

Introduction: Teachers Are Our Last and Best Hope   1

I. Positive Classroom Management

1. Moving Beyond Rules and Reactions   11

2. Teaching Basic Understandings: Limits
   and Courtesies   22

**II. Three Key Dimensions of Positive
    Classroom Management**

3. Setting Up a Safe and Productive Learning
   Environment   37

4. Teaching So Students Stay Focused and Learn   40

5. Managing a Smooth-Running Classroom   54

III. Blueprints for Success

6. Preparing Your Classroom   71

7. Reflective Practice for Better Teaching   87

Conclusion: Being Your Own Best Teacher   101

References   105

Suggested Readings   108

Index   110

Preface

Teachers need help. They want help, too. But they need and want the right kind of help. During my 25 years as an educator, I have seen how well teachers respond to help that is constructive, supportive, clear, and doable. This is especially true today. Our society—and our teachers—face challenges that were once not even imaginable. More strongly than ever, society is asking us to teach all students (advantaged and disadvantaged alike) to behave in a civilized, caring way and to help them realize their potential as adults. To accomplish this, society has given us classroom space, some lined paper, a few computers, and little else in managing the enormous job it has asked us to do.

Seventeen years ago, as a new principal seeking to help my teachers get a handle on classroom management, I found few resources on the subject. In response, I developed and taught a course for the Vermont State College system called "Managing and Understanding Children's Behavior." Since then, I have continued to develop and bring together ideas and materials to help teachers manage classrooms effectively, without resorting to methods that rob students of their dignity.

Although there are books and resources that deal with control in the classroom and enumerate ways to get students to behave, what makes this book different is the fact that it goes directly to what lies at the heart of all successfully managed classrooms. It goes past the threats, blame, rules, rewards, punishments, controls, and consequences. All of these are residue from well-meaning attempts by teachers to gain control of a classroom (usually, after it's out of control). My book highlights what effective teachers know after years of experience. They know that students need limits and structure, but in an active, productive environment. Students hear and internalize teachers' expectations not through dictates and mandates, but by virtue of the communication and discussion of basic understandings. Students flourish in classrooms that are places of activity and ideas, old and new.

In essence, effective teachers know that students can learn prosocial behavior—behavior that is beneficial not only to the individual, but to others, and to the larger society. Prosocial behavior is applicable, real-life behavior that students can take outside the classroom and use. Teachers can best teach students prosocial behavior through a system of positive classroom management.

These notions were confirmed recently by my analysis of responses from 105 teachers selected by the University of Vermont for their effective teaching and commitment to children and adolescents. I contacted each of these successful teachers and asked them to describe how they ran their classrooms. How, specifically, did they teach students good behavior? Almost to a person, their answers demonstrated a positive attitude and a belief in positive action. Every teacher believed that students could learn prosocial behavior. Furthermore, they spoke of the importance of action on their part. They held that teachers could and should teach, and—in their cases—were teaching students prosocial behavior.

My purpose in writing this book is to provide all teachers with concrete, practical, step-by-step guidance on becoming more effective in classroom management. Positive classroom management fosters prosocial student behavior and uses a proven approach that is positive and constructive rather than negative and punitive. Although most of my illustrations are geared toward teaching elementary and middle school grades, there is much here for high school teachers, preschool teachers, and, I dare say, even instructors in postsecondary schools. Our obligation to teach students prosocial behavior applies to all ages, preschool through college.

The introduction looks closely at why effective classroom management is absolutely necessary, and it describes the benefits of a positive, prosocial approach. Part I discusses classroom management and examines forces that work against prosocial behavior. Paradoxically, rules can actually be counterproductive to teaching students prosocial behavior.

Part II focuses on the practical aspects of three key dimensions of positive classroom management. The physical dimension encompasses how to set up the classroom to be a safe and productive learning environment. The instructional dimension section describes how to teach so that students stay focused and learn. The managerial dimension examines the nonteaching routines that are basic to a smooth-running classroom.

Part III offers a blueprint for successful classroom management using systematic preparation and reflection. Step-by-step checklists are included to help teachers prepare for the physical, managerial, and instructional dimensions of classroom management. The comprehensive summary of key points provided in the form of checklists can be used by a new teacher after first entering the empty classroom weeks before the students arrive, or by the experienced teacher who wants to review, evaluate, or more closely examine his or her practices. This book is written for all teachers, experienced and inexperienced, veteran and student. Excellence in teaching is developmental; it is not a fixed point. No excellent teacher ever felt she or he had little or nothing more to learn about teaching. Throughout our teaching careers we continue to work toward becoming the best teachers we can be.

Reflection plays a large part in that "becoming." The teacher who reflects on his or her actions has taken the first step toward resolving common difficulties that arise in teaching. Systematic reflection is essential to improving teaching effectiveness and meeting challenges of today's classrooms. Solutions to problems of classroom management are within the reach of every teacher who is willing to prepare, to follow through, and to reflect on the results. I know the ideas and strategies on these pages will be useful.

Acknowledgments

Several kind experts—experienced teachers and teacher educators "in the trenches"—generously furnished useful suggestions as I prepared this manuscript: Jennifer G. Harvey, teacher and member of the multiage team at the Crabapple Middle School in Roswell, Georgia; T. Paulette Quarrell, teacher of sixth grade social studies and English at Deming Junior High School in Deming, New Mexico; Professor John McFadden, Department of Teacher Education at California State University in Sacramento; Karleen Hamilton, who teaches at the El Rancho Structured School in Camarillo, California; and Chris Jakicic, principal of Willow Grove Elementary School in Buffalo Grove, Illinois.

Thoughtful advice was provided by Pat Mularchuk, a dear friend and master teacher. Pat is an exceptional teacher of exceptional education at MILA Elementary School in Merritt Island, Florida.

I deeply appreciate working with Corwin Press, a most professional publishing house. From the beginning, editor Ann McMartin was a delight to work with. She gave clear and intelligent feedback on my manuscript, and she handled requests with grace and dispatch.

S. Marlene Head, Toby Hopstone, and Susan McElroy have been very helpful as well. Speaking of professionalism, I am fortunate to work with an accomplished and supportive group of educators—my education department colleagues at Johnson State College in Vermont: Alice Whiting, Carol Story, Herb Tilley, Marilyn Page, Bruce Marlowe, Ken Brighton, Darlene Witte, Pat Eyler, Annamary Anderson, and Martha Vossler.

I am indebted to the 105 teachers cited for excellence by the University of Vermont. Their participation in my study shed additional light on how successful teachers manage their classrooms and teach students prosocial behavior. I am indebted, of course, to each of my many students over the years who have taught me so much.

I am particularly obliged to a stellar role model whose spirit remains with me. Early in life, I had the special inspiration of a master teacher, my aunt Flora Gigante. She was my godmother as well, and in our large extended family, she was its pride and joy. To my 5-year-old eyes, Aunt Flora was smart, stylish, and seemed to stand 7 feet tall!

One of the first Italian American women to be appointed to the principalship of a New York City public school, Aunt Flora was my hero. Each summer she traveled the world, bringing objects, ideas, and stories to her students (and nephew!) from Nepal, Sudan, the Falkland Islands, Mexico, and every other conceivable point on the globe. She brought me books and dreams. Most of all, Aunt Flora aroused my fascination with the world and my curiosity to experience it; to travel, to learn. Her enthusiasm for teaching others about this world was, literally, highly contagious.

A very practical woman, Aunt Flora would escort me around her Bronx, New York, public school, introducing me—politely and importantly—to her teachers, all the time privately pointing out to me what each teacher did well. She was a most positive educator: capable, strong, and, when necessary, tough. But even when she was tough, my aunt was never severe or vindictive. She was *positively tough*. I never heard my aunt blame or complain. She never criticized students or teachers, nor did she ever act victimized. Instead of pointing a finger of blame, Aunt Flora pointed to models of excellence, made clear her expectations, then worked toward what she valued. Her inspiration led me to teaching, and I have not once regretted that decision.

About the Author

Robert DiGiulio is an education professor at Johnson State College in Vermont. He earned his Ph.D. in human development and education from the University of Connecticut and his B.A. and M.S. in education from St. John's University. He began his teaching career in the New York City public school system, where he taught for a number of years. His 25-year career as an educator includes teaching at the elementary, middle, junior high, and college levels, with experience ranging from crowded urban schools to a one-room schoolhouse. He has also served as an elementary school principal, educational researcher, consultant, and writer.

As an educational consultant, Dr. DiGiulio codeveloped "TeenTest," a vocational counseling program for adolescents. He also coauthored educational computer software called *Language Activities Courseware* and authored its teacher's guide. His *Teacher* magazine article "The 'Guaranteed' Behavior Improvement Plan" was recognized as having one of the highest total readership scores of any of its articles.

Dr. DiGiulio has authored numerous books including *When You Are a Single Parent, Effective Parenting, Beyond Widowhood,* and *After*

Loss, selected by Reader's Digest as their featured condensed book in May 1994. He is a contributing author to *The Oxford Companion to Women's Writing in the United States* and *Marriage and Family in a Changing Society* and is the coauthor of *Straight Talk About Death and Dying.*

His research interests lie in human development and education, including human survival, parenting and teaching styles, and classroom management. Dr. DiGiulio resides with his wife and children in northern Vermont.

Introduction

Teachers Are Our Last and Best Hope

THE headlines almost scream at us: "Our schools are failing," "Our students do more poorly than students in other countries," "Teacher training needs reform," "Parents give teachers little support." No day passes without our hearing or reading despairing words about the state of education and our schools. Despite their ominous tones and politically correct cynicism, there's really nothing new about these types of reports. They are timeless. The report of the New Hampshire public schools for the year 1853 (New Hampshire Board of Education) revealed a remarkably similar public opinion. In 1853, too many students dropped out, and too few behaved well or gave much effort to their studies. The school day was fragmented, filled with too many subjects and too much "hurry and confusion" (p. 21). In 1853, teachers were poorly trained, poorly paid, and overwhelmed by their duties. School boards held students and teachers most responsible for this state of affairs, yet they also roundly castigated parents for doing a poor job of child rearing, specifically in teaching good behavior and etiquette. Nothing new there!

Indeed, the persons blamed back in 1853—students, parents, and teachers—are the very same ones who continue to be blamed for the present dismal state of our schools! The truth is that blaming has not helped the state of education over the past 150 years.

1

Blaming prevents us from taking constructive action toward resolution of a problem.

This applies to all parties in the "blame game": students, parents, and teachers. Take, for example, how we blame students. It is especially odd for teachers to blame students. Even if given the least capable of students, our business is to teach them, not judge them. Our job is to arouse curiosity, not condemn indifference. If a student truly cannot learn, then what use can a teacher possibly be? If kids are born unteachable, how can teachers justify their jobs? (It is like the joke about the psychiatrist who dismissed his patient with the words "I can't help you. You're crazy!")

Parents are also popular targets for censure. A recent Harris survey of more than 1,000 teachers revealed that the largest majority of teachers (71%) agreed that "lack of parental supervision at home" was a "major factor" contributing to school violence (Metropolitan Life Insurance Company [MLIC], 1993, pp. 35-38). The teachers' perceptions may be entirely accurate. Yes, there are unfit parents. Even so, blaming parents is just as fruitless as blaming students, for if students we see in school seem to be desperately lost and are acting out, imagine how poorly their parents' lives are progressing! It is a waste of time to blame parents, and it is equally unrealistic to await some government program that will suddenly and markedly improve the quality of life for millions of children—or for their teachers. Despite years of studies, commissions, blue-ribbon panels, and fervid talk about educational "restructuring," education and teachers are still not a national priority, perhaps even less so than in 1853.

Then who is to blame? Politicians? Other countries? Bad luck? None of the above, because blame—no matter how accurately it appears to be directed—still gets us nowhere. Blaming prevents us from taking constructive action toward resolution of a problem. What works?

Taking charge of what we can change does work, and it
works spectacularly.

When I first heard feelings of desperation and cynicism expressed
by my fifth-grade inner-city students many years ago, I was taken
aback. Like other middle-class teachers I was surprised by their wrath
and their view of the world as a bad, dangerous place. Like all child
victims, they blamed themselves for their poverty and their disadvantaged lot in life.

I felt their pain, but despite my frustration with a social and
political system that I believed perpetuated this underclass, I felt
strongly that answers—to their victimization, to their anger, to their
antisocial behaviors—had to come from within each of us. We had to
start changing the world right in our classrooms. Changes would be
local—starting small and letting it grow. I also realized that the bur-
den of responsibility was on the teacher—me. As the only one in the
classroom with even a modicum of power, I had to use it wisely, to
provide leadership and an impetus for change. They desperately
needed a model—something different from what they knew outside of
school. Moreover, that model had to be real and tangible. Words alone
were inadequate. I had to plan, work toward, and create a classroom
environment that exemplified the type of world I spoke to them
about. I had to back up my words with action. Although I never
worked so hard in my life as I did my first 5 years in teaching, I
quickly learned that taking charge of what could be changed got
results. Several years later, in my first position as school principal,
and after 4 years of hard work by our entire school staff, our elementary school (in one of the poorest towns in the state) was identified
as a School With Exemplary Discipline by Phi Delta Kappa's Com-
mission on Discipline at Ohio State University.

My experience is far from unique or unusual. Many of the teachers who were recently selected and honored by the University of
Vermont for their teaching excellence and their commitment to

children described their work modestly. They did not see what they did as highly unusual, but they did share the belief that all students could do well and that what the teacher did was pivotal to each student's success (DiGiulio, 1994).

Done well, teaching is a hard job. Any successful teacher knows that teaching is labor-intensive. Teachers make more evaluation-related decisions during their workday than members of any other occupation or profession, even more than physicians or air traffic controllers. Teachers must constantly be thinking on their feet, taking in information, processing it, and making decisions that are in the best interests of the students.

Teaching is also time-intensive: The workload does not end at dismissal time! Indeed, teaching demands more time spent in preparation than any other profession or occupation. The preparation is ongoing, just like a holiday meal. I remember my parents spending days preparing for our Thanksgiving dinners: deciding what to serve, thinking about previous holiday meals, going over the list of guests (usually ranging in number from 10 to 20), determining where to seat people, and so forth. My parents then went into action, furiously cleaning, shopping, cooking, baking, and, once the guests arrived, serving the meal. I remember what the house looked like when it was all over. My parents would collapse, exhausted, on the downstairs chairs and sofa. The next day they would reflect on it all—what went well and what might be improved for next time.

Teaching involves a similar process, only it is harder in at least two ways. First, teachers always have 20 to 30 "guests" at each "meal." Second, the guests keep coming back, day after day for almost 200 consecutive Thanksgivings!

The hardest part is not in teaching subject matter; it is managing a classroom. National Education Association polls of teacher opinion typically show "managing classroom discipline" as the teachers' most pressing and often-mentioned challenge. Indeed, the public is also concerned about classroom management. In the annual Gallup Polls of the Public's Attitudes Toward The Public Schools, "discipline" typically leads the list of problems facing our schools. (The Gallup Poll appears each September in *Phi Delta Kappan*.)

Indeed, there are some very practical reasons why teachers (and future teachers) should be concerned about how well their classrooms operate. The first and most basic reason is that student learning and achievement are at stake. Research clearly shows that students learn more—and they learn more efficiently—in smooth-running classrooms. In a recent analysis of 50 years of educational research, of the 28 factors evaluated, classroom management had the greatest effect on school achievement. Working from a database of 11,000 findings, the authors concluded that classroom management affected learning more than factors such as home environment, cognitive processes, school climate, school policies, and parental support (Wang, Haertel, & Walberg, 1993/1994).

In addition to research, common sense tells us that a chaotic classroom distracts students, preventing them from attending, focusing, and concentrating. Disorder wastes time and hinders students from reaching their educational potential. Chaotic settings prevent students from reaching their social potential as well. In a disruptive classroom environment, it is unlikely that a child or teen can learn much about how to treat others respectfully.

Second, a well-run classroom makes your job easier, and it makes teaching possible. When teaching is possible, we feel a sense of accomplishment. No teacher ever felt a sense of accomplishment while suffocated by an unruly, tumultuous classroom.

Third, your job is at stake. Whether or not you think it's fair, your effectiveness as a teacher will largely be determined by how well you manage a classroom. Indeed, difficulty with classroom management drives many teachers into other professions. Aside from—and in addition to—dissatisfaction with a low salary, lack of discipline by students is the most frequently mentioned reason given by teachers who are thinking of leaving teaching and by former teachers who have actually left (MLIC, 1986, pp. 19-20).

Fourth, you could be the defendant in a lawsuit. No teacher has yet been successfully sued for educational malpractice (a student's failure to learn), yet teachers have been sued successfully (held personally liable for monetary damages) when plaintiffs' lawyers convinced a judge or jury that a student's injury was due to teacher negligence. Of course, some student injuries are unforeseeable, and unforeseeable serious injury can happen in the best-run classrooms headed by experienced teachers. Nonetheless, teachers who create and maintain a safe and orderly environment for students will be in an advantageous position when they must defend themselves in court.

Finally, our society needs it desperately! A teacher's leadership and influence have never been more consequential. Although parents and religious leaders still shape prosocial behavior, schools are being asked to shoulder more of this responsibility than ever before. Whether we agree with it or not, this new responsibility has increasingly trickled down to become part of each teacher's job. In a free society like ours, the stakes are high. Indeed, except for trial lawyers, today's teachers are the only professionals our society has—and will have in the future—who stand between a student and jail. If students fail to learn prosocial behavior, their misbehavior and antisocial behavior soon become matters for the legal system and, ultimately, prison.

Aggravating this predicament is the increasing isolation brought about by technology. In the 1960s, media experts enthusiastically predicted that television would create a global village, bringing us closer together. They told us that "electronic technology fosters and encourages unification and involvement" (McLuhan & Fiore, 1967, pp. 8, 67). Quite the opposite seems to have occurred: Television has insulated and isolated us.

It has also shaped our experiences, even when we are not watching. When we do meet to talk we have less in common. This is so because our experiences (what we watch on TV) are increasingly unique. In 1954, just about everyone with a TV watched *I Love Lucy*, and talked about each show afterward, but today, with hundreds of simultaneous TV program choices, what you view is very likely to be different from what your friends and neighbors view.

Because it demands a viewer's total attention, television does not allow for human interaction, and its content rarely emphasizes prosocial behavior. Indeed, since the 1950s the content of television has become increasingly violent. Children imitate aggressive and violent behavior they view on TV (National Institute of Mental Health, 1982), and they carry those behaviors into adulthood (Zuckerman & Zuckerman, 1985).

Furthermore, television occupies a huge chunk of our students' time. A recent Harris survey of teachers and students revealed that public school students spend much of their time watching television. On school days, most students watch at least 2 to 3 hours of television, and one out of four watch at least 4 or 5 hours per school day (MLIC, 1993, p. 31). Watching television for 5 hours per day for 1 year is the equivalent of over 2-1/2 months of nonstop watching!

Because of increased isolation brought about by television watching, along with the likelihood that both parents work outside the home and the decline of the influence of extended families and organized religion, among other factors, school not only remains a good place for teaching and reinforcing students' prosocial behavior; it has now become, in many wealthy and poor school districts alike, the only place students will learn prosocial behavior.

Think about the simple act of eating together. In many American homes today, between the end of school and bedtime, it's only the child, a microwave oven, and television. As a result, school mealtimes are, for millions of children, the only opportunity they have to eat with others and the only chance they will have to learn how to behave during a meal.

Researchers at the Harvard School of Public Health analyzed the results from 20 years of studies on child behavior (Buka & Earls, 1993). They found that behavior problems in early childhood are the strongest predictors of violent and antisocial behavior later in life. In looking at teenage and adult subjects who as children participated in programs such as Head Start, one researcher reported that social skills learned in childhood are durable. Prosocial skills learned by adolescents when they were children in Head Start stayed with them even if their academic gains eventually faded (Whitmire, 1994). There is little question that time and effort that teachers spend in teaching children prosocial behavior are investments in the future.

The bottom line is worth repeating. Teachers may be our last, best, and perhaps only real hope for addressing the more serious social issues that face our society: respecting human differences, honoring human dignity, and ensuring our survival as a people.

The good news is that running an effective prosocial classroom is within reach of all teachers. The techniques and skills can be learned. Those educators who learn them will be prized. In fact, I believe that over the next 10 to 20 years those who can teach students prosocial behavior will become as valued as doctors in a plague.

I

Positive Classroom Management

1

Moving Beyond Rules and Reactions

BEFORE speaking about specific strategies useful in class management and encouraging prosocial behavior, I want to briefly examine the whole idea of classroom management.

In its most positive sense, classroom management means a great deal more than "making kids behave." It means, essentially, the teacher getting things going, keeping things moving, keeping things safe, and running the show well enough to be able to actually teach and have students learn. At its heart, positive classroom management is creative: It creates both the best situation in which the student can learn and the teacher can teach. At its worst, classroom management is negative and adversarial: Teacher is pitted against student, and students are pitted against one another and the teacher. The sad truth is that the needs of the learner and those of the teacher are not naturally at odds. Teaching and learning need not be a "zero-sum" game. One side does not have to lose so that the other side can win. Yet when classroom management is not working, constructive and creative teacher action is replaced by teacher reaction and adversarial behavior.

Why does this happen? Why do teachers react as adversaries to students? Because teachers are human. Under stress, humans instinctively fear losing control. Faced with a highly stressful classroom situation, choices get quickly narrowed down to two. A teacher can either cave in, give in, and be perceived as ineffectual, or a teacher can dig in, come down hard, and resort to harsh, reactive methods to try to restore order.

On one hand, teachers may become slaves to fear. Fear is a normal human reaction when facing the unknown or unfamiliar. For some teachers, a new classroom full of faces is as strange as a dark cave filled with bats. Faced with the need to prepare, plan, carry out, organize, prioritize, and evaluate, some teachers are overwhelmed. They simply do not know what to do or where to begin. There is nothing wrong with them. They simply have not yet learned how to positively and constructively manage the classroom.

On the other hand, some teachers adopt a "get tough" approach. These classroom management approaches, which attempt to subdue students with rules, threats, and punishments, can't teach them good behavior. Some "assertive" classroom management packages rely heavily on punishment and other external controls—checks placed on a chalkboard or marbles in a jar. In such packaged plans, the teacher is promoting not prosocial behavior but conformity to impersonal rules. Students may momentarily comply for fear of punishment, yet the "good behavior" these plans produce is short-lived. Because the temporary good behavior has not been internalized, it will not carry over to other settings such as the school yard or lunchroom. Worst of all, these plans can turn a teacher into a dizzy robot whose time and attention are more focused on detecting and reacting than on teaching.

At the other extreme, a laissez-faire classroom management approach, which provides students with no structure or guidance, may be just as detrimental to student dignity as overregulation. Anyone can "give kids freedom" by permitting students to do whatever pleases them. Remember that children and teens need to feel safe in school if they are to learn, and that safety includes protection from being harmed by other students. All students need freedom of choice and to experience empowerment—to have some control over what they are learning—yet this must occur within the context of a structured and secure learning environment. Consequently, classroom management must be prosocial: It must promote students' healthy social and emotional development in a secure environment. Ultimately, classroom management must teach students how to have their needs met without resorting to dishonesty or violence to themselves or others.

Managing a Business Versus Managing a Classroom

Some teachers mistrust the word *management*, thinking it implies unfair power manipulations. Because we hear all too often how power is abused by government and business leaders, teachers can be uncomfortable using power to manage a classroom. What I am suggesting is that teachers need to use their power, but in a way different from the way it is used in business.

Compare the business world to teaching. The goals are different: In business, the goal is profit. The goal of schooling is not profit but the education of all children. Just as goals differ, so too do the means differ to achieve those goals. To achieve its goals, business often uses coercion: threats of reduced pay or even ultimately firing those who do not produce or measure up to a work standard. Whereas businesses can and do fire employees, who may simply go to work elsewhere, public schools cannot fire failing students. These students must stay, relegated to a second-class existence as "poor students," "troublemakers," and "losers." These labels stick, residing within the student's self-concept long after the student has dropped out or left school.

Although some school reformers have suggested that "schools should be run like businesses," the problem, ironically, is just that: Schools *have* been run like businesses. Each day countless well-meaning teachers use the same reward and coercion techniques as are used in business: techniques that do not work. Educators who habitually use these techniques wind up abusing their power by "firing" students (through the use of failure and overreliance on suspension).

To summarize: Whereas the "bottom line" of a corporation is monetary profit for the benefit of that corporation, the "bottom line" of a school is the education of students for the benefit of both the individual student and the larger society. Hence, schools' methods toward achieving those goals must be prosocial. Failed businesses end up in a bankruptcy court's filing cabinet, but educationally and socially bankrupt students do not so easily disappear.

The Mythical Power of Rules

As we attempt to move toward a more appropriate (and positive) use of power in managing the classroom, there is one huge stumbling block that must first be recognized: our passion for rules. As a society, we love laws. We take it for granted that laws protect us and are necessary for civilized society to exist. Similarly, our schools love rules. Teachers take it for granted that rules are an essential element of any classroom management plan. But think about this: Human civilizations that have survived longest are those with no formal legal systems. The Netsilik Eskimos of northern Canada, for example, have thrived under inhospitable conditions for 10,000 years without formal or written laws or rules. The Netsilik have relied on three central yet unwritten codes of conduct: collaboration, wherein all work together hunting, preparing, and sharing food; kinship, the maintenance of a network of ties to nuclear and extended family; and patterned relationships, the forming of partnerships ("dyads") that bring unrelated people together in an almost impossibly hostile Arctic world (Balikci, 1970, chaps. 3-6). Behavior beneficial to the society is taught personally, through codes of conduct. To "enforce" these codes of conduct, Netsilik rely not on courts or prisons, but on social pressure. Membership in society is valued, thus being ostracized is a potent force. Without having to label its members as either "law-abiding" or "criminals," Netsilik promote behavior that is both productive to the individual and to the Netsilik as a whole. In a word, it is a prosocial system.

Laws and rules may be necessary in huge, anonymous, complex societies, but are inappropriate in the smaller world of a classroom of teachers and students. Like the Netsilik system, the classroom works best when it works as a small and simple society. Unfortunately, many teachers assume that, because rules and laws are part of our larger "real" world, they must compose the heart of their classroom management system. Yet laws are a "necessary evil" of the real world: Because our larger society is so huge and complex, it cannot use person-to-person, Netsilik-type understandings (handshakes don't seal agreements any longer!). Instead, it relies on a complex and formalized law system of police, lawyers, courts, and prisons, and even these expensive measures are of questionable effectiveness.[1]

However, precisely because classrooms are not huge and complex societies, we teachers have a substantial advantage: We can take a "small society" approach to classroom management. By erroneously adopting a "larger society" approach, we set up ways to identify and punish "criminality" but rarely get down to teaching good behavior. It is only within the "small society" classroom that we can establish basic understandings. There, through interaction that is person-to-person, we can discuss, set, and practice limits, and ultimately, teach students prosocial behavior. Unless we move toward the "small society" classroom, prosocial behavior cannot be taught or learned no matter how much money is spent or how long we extend the school day or school year. As a necessary first step, before we can in fact teach prosocial behavior, we must think about—and reevaluate—our misguided love affair with rules.

Schools Without Rules: Why Rules Are a Dead End

Perhaps the biggest drawback to relying on rules in school is that rules do not prevent misbehavior—rather, they invite it. Like a ticking time bomb, we await the first infraction. In a rules system, something bad must first occur. Our legal system can proceed to trial only after something occurred that is suspected to have been illegal! Until evidence is available of their violation, rules and laws are powerless and, in effect, meaningless.

In fact, rules create more problems than they solve. The United States has more laws than the rest of the world combined, and government makes use of those laws: The United States has a higher percentage of its population in prison than any other industrialized nation. Over 1 million Americans are now in prison (Beck & Bonczar, 1994). Including the 440,000 Americans awaiting trial or serving terms of less than 1 year, that means that one out of every 180 Americans is now in prison! The system keeps getting more efficient. Over the past 10 years, the number of prisoners has more than doubled.

Yes, our law system efficiently identifies criminals, yet in doing so, it creates a colossal problem: What to do with these identified criminals? Once we have called them "criminals," there's only one thing to do: build prisons. As the number of criminals grows (as it has), so must the number of prisons. Whereas this is an enormous, expensive, stopgap arrangement for society, in schools "crime-and-punishment" becomes an impossible method: What can schools do with students who are the school's identified "criminals"? Schools have no alternative other than putting them out—suspension and expulsion. It is not farfetched to say that the more students that are suspended and expelled, the fewer schools we need, but the fewer schools we have, the more prisons we will need.

In effect, punishments actually exempt students from learning prosocial behavior. Conventional wisdom tells us that punishment (or at least the threat of it) is a necessity in teaching students good behavior, but think about it: Punishment or the threat of punishment actually sabotages the process. Punishment actually relieves the student from an obligation to behave prosocially. In a rules system, students have this choice: "Don't break the rule, or break it and take the punishment." Students can thus trade their willingness to suffer punishment for their duty to respect one another. The only thing that a teacher can do in response is to raise the stakes by making the punishment increasingly distasteful in the hope that fewer will opt for it. In reality, prosocial behavior must be understood to be obligatory, not a choice or an option. Certainly, you can (and should) provide your students with many choices during the school day, but prosocial behavior is a goal that all of us—teachers and students—must work toward. Because it is necessary for individual and group survival, no one can buy out of that obligation, nor "cop a plea" or be let off the hook. (Remember the Netsilik?) In a classroom, prosocial behavior is a standard for all, practiced until it is learned, not until someone tires of it or opts for punishment.

Ironically, rules protect students from the natural consequences of their behavior and misbehavior. Instead of laying out prefabricated consequences ahead of time, which rule-based classroom management programs tell you to do, plan for consequences to be as natural as possible. Let them flow from the specific situation. Natural consequences emphasize the student's responsibility to carry out his or her job, instead of emphasizing the teacher's responsibility to react and be "the enforcer."

For example, a typical rule that protects students from the natural consequences of their behavior might be "Three missed homeworks equals losing one recess period." In response to this rule, you will definitely hear a student reason "If the limit is three, then two missed homeworks are permitted, right?" In fairness, of course, you must agree to that notion, but instead of waiting for each student's third missed homework assignment, instead of allowing 50 missed homeworks in a class of 25, instead of having that rule at all, you should hold students accountable for each homework. Thus, when John misses his first homework assignment, he must account for it. Ask him about it. Instead of establishing a rule that gives blanket permission for students to miss two homeworks, let students know that even one will not be forgotten: "You have to bring it in." In this fashion, students are confronted with their own realities, a consequence that is truly consequential to each student. Naturally, if there is a student with a chronic problem, I would take further steps, possibly involving the parents in a daily report card to help ensure the homework is completed, but I would never allow a rule to protect students from being accountable for all of their work.

Children do not learn good behavior from rules. Research tells us that children do not see laws and rules as guides to good behavior. Written and verbal rules and laws are too abstract for young children (they take them literally and keep them external to their thinking). Rules are also external to older children and preteens, who internalize them as their social relationships develop, modifying them to the circumstances at hand (Reimer, Paolitto, & Hersh, 1983, pp. 39-42).

Besides, children see morality (doing the right thing) as justice. They do not interpret morality as adherence to rules. Ask a 4-year-old if it's all right to hit other children. Most will say, "No, it's not." Ask if it would be all right to hit if there was a rule that allowed hitting. Because a child sees the basic injustice in hitting and being hit, the child would still say that—even if their school permitted hitting other children—hitting others is wrong (Shweder, Turiel, & Much, 1981). Although a child naturally sees the injustice of hitting, the actual prosocial behavior itself, both in form and frequency, must be taught and must be learned (Eisenberg & Mussen, 1989, p. 6). We cannot passively rely on a child's natural empathic feelings or sense of justice to automatically develop into good behavior!

Nor should we go to the other extreme and resort to drastic measures. Although some teachers use threats of punishment to scare students into doing or not doing something, young people do not learn prosocial behavior through threats. Children and teens learn prosocial behavior from their own experiences with their environment (things), from their experiences with others (people), and from within themselves, as part of their growing ability to empathize with and to feel for others. For instance, upon being himself hit by another, any 5-year-old instantly knows injustice—he knows hitting others is not right, regardless of the existence of written or verbal rules against (or for) hitting. Even if an adult were to say "you deserved it" (based on the "eye-for-an-eye" law), the child's sense of justice is unmoved: "Nobody should be hit. Nobody has a right to hit other children." (How sad it is when we see a child who does believe "I deserved it.")

Ultimately, rules short-circuit a child's natural sense of justice. This does not come from outside the child (rules) but develops inside the child (empathy). By age 11 months, most children are capable of empathy—caring responses to others, especially others in distress. In his summary of literature on children's prosocial behavior, Hoffman (1979) found that empathic responses to others arise before the first year of life and that prosocial behavior toward others can be learned and carried out by children as young as 2 years of age.

Another inherent problem with rules as teaching tools is that they are usually expressed in the negative. It's one thing to have a rule ("No swearing allowed"), but it is another matter to actually and concretely teach students how to express themselves constructively. It's one thing to say "No running during a fire drill," but it is an entirely different matter to actually demonstrate to students how and where to walk during a fire drill, and then have them practice it.

Rules cannot instill respect for others, or for others' property. There is the familiar expression "Locks are meant for honest people." What this phrase says is how deceptive the preventive benefit of locks truly is. Anyone who has lived in a large city (as I have) and has had his apartment broken into (as I have) despite locks on doors (and yes, even on my windows) knows this truth: Those who are intent upon stealing my stereo will not be deterred by a lock, whereas those with no interest in stealing would not even notice that my door and windows are locked. In both cases, it is the presence or absence of an interest in stealing that drives the behavior, not the presence or absence of a lock.

We teachers must avoid creating more locks (rules). We must teach to transform the attitude that fuels the behavior ("the interest in stealing"), and not to "the presence of the lock" (rules and penalties).

This is not as difficult as it may seem. When you attend your cousin's wedding reception, you are not given a list of rules of behavior. It is understood (remember the Netsilik?) that among other things you will not steal Aunt Peggy's purse and that you will behave prosocially. Even if you may not have a strong liking for your relatives, you are expected to show civility toward them. You actually do so because you have already internalized the limits to the situation, even if this is your first wedding reception. You have learned the limits elsewhere but can transfer them to this situation. Successful prosocial classroom managers replicate that idea in the classroom by expecting civil behavior, even toward those one dislikes.

Rules can give a teacher a false sense of security. A classroom I visited as a principal provides an illustration. Above the chalkboard was a banner the width of the classroom. It was a list of ten rules, printed in huge boldface uppercase letters. The teacher was puzzled when, by October 1, her class was out of control. She clearly posted the rules and said she even involved students in coming up with the list.

What was wrong with this?

One thing: As I sat to discuss this with her, she realized that she never got around to actually teaching her students how to behave. Like many other teachers she assumed that rules spoke for themselves. ("After all," she said, "I made the rules clear. I posted them in big letters, too!")

Rules foster a distorted sense of justice. Rules transform any clever student into a "classroom lawyer," engaging the teacher in arguments over the meaning of classroom or school rules. Although this may sharpen a student's debating skills, it serves as a diversion from learning prosocial behavior. Worse, students can develop a distorted idea of justice: If you argue successfully, then no law has been broken! (We read of public figures, accused of some crime, flatly denying wrongdoing. In our "innocent-until-proven-guilty" nation, the accused is always technically correct in proclaiming his innocence!) By arguing skillfully, many who have behaved wrongly are found not guilty.

Our legal system is a poor model for the prosocial classroom teacher and student. Learning prosocial behavior demands that teachers shift students' focus away from arguing *why* (their side of a story) to considering *what* (their action) did to another:

Punching another child is wrong, even if there were no witnesses. Punching another child is wrong, even if you can produce witnesses who say she first swore at you. Punching another child is wrong, even if he first punched you.

Finally, an overemphasis on laws and rules degrades us as a society. Recently I stopped my car at a rest area off Interstate 95 in Laurel, Maryland. As I got out of my car and walked toward the concession building, I was struck by the size and number of signs all around me: "NO PARKING," "KEEP OUT," "ONE WAY," "YIELD," "STOP," "KEEP OFF THE GRASS." As I turned I saw a beautiful hillside opposite the building. On that hillside were posted monstrous brown signs, as huge as billboards:

NO TRESPASSING
STATE HIGHWAY AUTHORITY

To the right, another: "NO TRESPASSING. STATE HIGHWAY AUTHORITY." And another, and another. (Ironically, as evidenced by well-worn paths under the billboards, people still "trespassed" and walked on the grass. So much for "locks!")

Whether at a public rest area or in a public school classroom, rules—posted large—are, by themselves, signs of desperation. In our classrooms, bigger and more menacing signs cannot teach students prosocial behavior. Only we teachers can teach prosocial behavior.

If Not Rules, What?

Before you think I'm advocating anarchy in the classroom, let me restate: Successful teachers may have rules, but, for the reasons discussed earlier, they do not depend on rules to do the teaching. Experienced, successful teachers (including my sample of Vermont's "outstanding teachers") avoid crime-and-punishment classroom management.

Instead, they establish basic understandings for prosocial behavior before the fact, not after misbehavior has occurred. (One teacher said that "Each school year begins with an in-depth discussion of the term 'respect' and all that it entails in our classroom." Another wrote that "We spend a lot of time in class talking about, demonstrating, and highlighting appropriate behavior.") Experienced and successful teachers also discuss—and set—limits. They then actually and concretely teach students prosocial behavior. (A third teacher advised: "Model respectful, caring behavior for your students and directly teach the skills—don't assume or leave it to chance.") But what attitudes, knowledge, and skills do successful teachers actually teach? What is their alternative to relying on rules? The answer is that they establish basic understandings at a personal level.

Note

1. In their analysis of the increase in violence in America, a team of public health researchers stated that traditional criminal justice responses are simply not working: "America's predominant response to violence has been a reactive one—to pour resources into deterring and incapacitating violent offenders by apprehending, arresting, adjudicating, and incarcerating them through the criminal justice system. This approach, however, has not made an appreciable difference. Although the average prison time served for violent crime in the United States tripled between 1975 and 1989, there was no concomitant decrease in the level of violent crimes" (Mercy, Rosenberg, Powell, Broome, & Roper, 1993).

2

Teaching Basic Understandings
Limits and Courtesies

ALMOST 100 years ago, French sociologist Emile Durkheim said that in order for children to learn prosocial behavior, they must first be oriented toward the well-being of others, or what he called "collectivity." "Moral behavior," he wrote, "demands an inclination toward collectivity" (Durkheim, 1925/1961, p. 233). Before we can teach children *how* to behave well, we must first instill in them *a desire* (inclination) to behave well. Durkheim emphasized that this inclination does not happen automatically. It must be taught; it must be learned. Although he did acknowledge the significance of family and home, Durkheim felt that teachers and schools were in the most advantageous position to foster prosocial behavior—"moral behavior" toward others.

But which "moral behaviors" should we teachers foster, and how can we do so without relying on rules? As we think about both questions, let's "get real"; let's look at real people in the real world. (Keep in mind Durkheim's term *inclination*.) When you go to the post office to purchase stamps, for example, you practice a hundred different prosocial behaviors, from trivial to significant: waiting in line, keeping your voice moderate, asking for stamps, and so on. In normal, mundane situations like these you do not consult (or need to consult) any list of rules of prosocial behavior. Once you are actually in the situation at the post office, you are not compelled to respect others (you will not get arrested for not waiting in line), but you are *inclined* toward the welfare of others. You *want* to behave well. You are inclined because you are aware of—you have learned—the limits and courtesies appropriate to that social situation. Limits are boundaries; courtesies are what we do and say.

Limits at the post office include your standing behind (and not ahead of) the last person in line once you arrive. Limits keep you from bypassing the line and directly approaching the window. Limits also depend on the setting. For example, I do not belch loudly on line in the post office as I might walking alone in the woods, nor do I use vulgarity or a loud voice in speaking to another.

Courtesies are how we treat others. Courtesies are how we show empathy—that we recognize that other people have feelings and sensibilities. If an elderly man or woman is struggling to open the door, I will leave the line to open the door. You will let me back in line when I return from opening the door for them. If you trip over my briefcase, I say words to tell you how I feel (for example, "Sorry!") and words to tell you how I hope you are feeling (for example, "Are you okay?").

Keep in mind that there is no rule or law referring to any of these behaviors. You and I are aware of post office limits and courtesies solely because we have already learned them not from lists of rules, but from our prior experiences with other people in other settings notably, home and school. Schools (and the media) have done well in teaching about diversity—how we differ—but prosocial behavior means that students must also learn about likeness, especially (and most urgently) that others who live in and share our world have needs and feelings. As I said before, in the small society of the classroom students can see, hear, and become sensitive to others' feelings and needs. When our students (with our guidance) develop within themselves an inclination toward the collective good, they become capable of prosocial behavior every time they step into a post office, or museum, mall, synagogue, or supermarket.

Limits are needed by all children and adolescents, who will continue to need them as prosocial adults. In the classroom (as elsewhere), limits are boundaries. Because they are boundaries, limits must be clear, concise, and concrete. For example, what is a workable classroom noise level? Where may we go after lunch? Do we bounce a basketball in the classroom? If not, where may we do so?

A few key limits and routines must be established the very first day of school, and students must practice them daily during the first week. Examples include limits of personal space and personal property. (Checklists II and III in Chapter 6 provide more details.)

Once key limits and routines are in place, we teach limits best by discussion, by talking to and with our students. This allows students to revise and update their previous conceptions of prosocial behavior. Take this 4th-grade discussion:

> "Last year Mrs. Marsh said we could bring water guns to class. I brought mine!"
> "Did being able to bring a water gun make students happy, Mark?"
> "Yeah! When you 'got somebody good'!" (all laugh)
> "But what about the kid who gets hit? Steve, did you ever get squirted?"
> "Yeah! In the back of Mrs. Marsh's class, three kids ganged up on me all at once! Pete got me right in the face. . . . "
> "Did you think it was fun?"
> "Well, sorta. No, I guess it was . . . embarrassing?"
> "Mike?"
> "I shot at my brother, but then he got so mad he threw a glass of water in my face and then I got so mad I punched him."
> "Angela?"
> "Steve got moved at lunch yesterday. Everyone kept laughing at him after he got squirted right in his ear . . . ."

Note the process. Note the basic understandings being established:

---

1. **Being a target isn't fun.**
2. **Humiliation is painful.**
3. **It makes us want to strike back.**

Also note how rich this is, how it can incline students toward the good of others, and how different it is from a teacher's making and posting of rules.

What is perhaps most powerful about establishing basic understandings is that teachers do not have to go through this process with every single item or issue. Students can—and will—generalize (extend) the basic understandings that are established. By extending them, students can apply them to other situations. If it is understood that being a target is not fun, students can apply it to other areas, such as group teasing, picking on a student, or ridiculing someone in front of others.

Take the second basic understanding: Humiliation is painful. Note how limits flow naturally from this simple basic understanding: No using toys to humiliate others. Water guns have no real purpose other than humiliation, so leave them home. (Extension: Other toys used to humiliate should be left home, too.) Perhaps a most relevant extension students can be encouraged to embrace is one especially important limit, given the urgent situation in too many contemporary schools:

---

humiliation = pain = no water guns = no guns

Rules, metal detectors, security guards, or police dogs can never teach the previously mentioned limit.

In addition to limits, courtesies are also part of the classroom's basic understandings. Courtesies are words and actions used to regard and treat other persons humanely. Courtesies are a sign of consideration of others. Courtesies allow us to communicate when an error has been made. If I bump into a student, courtesies give me words to help the student understand I did not mean to do it, and they give me words to convey that I feel bad about any pain he may have suffered. Courtesies also give the student words to let me know that he or she is not hurt or angry. Like limits, courtesies must be taught actually and concretely; not only discussed but practiced within the classroom. As with limits, they flow from a basic understanding that bumping another can be painful.

More Basic Understandings: A Prosocial Prescription

Here is a "starter list" of four basic understandings. This list (or one you develop) will form the core of discussion, and it will also serve as a teacher's guide for you. Over the course of the school year, more basic understandings can and should be added and addressed. (These can also be used as a starter list for your school to establish in each classroom.)

1. *Respect Is Nonnegotiable.* All students are to be respected: by each other, by the teacher, and vice versa. This is a cornerstone of all basic understandings for prosocial behavior. Hurting or insulting others, for example, is wrong because one forsakes respect of and for other human beings.

Examples of Prosocial Discussion: Is vulgar language ever allowed? When? (limit). Is it to be directed at another? (limit and courtesy). Is it okay to treat someone badly? When? (limits and courtesies). As a third-grade example:

> "My mom's boyfriend Roy uses really bad words. 'Specially when he's mad."
> "Yeah. I know what you mean. My brother is, like, always saying bad words."
> "Gina, how do you feel about it when it happens?"
> "Terrible! I tell him to 'shut up' and so does Mom!"
> "Wow. I can't tell my 'Uncle Roy' to shut up so I just walk into the other room."
> "How can we be sure things are different in our classroom? Jamal?"
> "We can't walk away, can we? We gotta stay in this room. Don't we?"
> "Alexis?"
> "We don't have to walk away if everybody treats everybody right. Have everybody be nice to each other. To say bad words only when they are by themselves, or outside, or when nobody can hear . . . ."
> "And, we can just talk to each other when we're mad, and say 'I'm not happy with something' instead of saying bad words behind somebody's back."
> "What about 'shut up'? Jamal?"

"We can't say 'shut up'—that's rude. Nobody should say it if
everybody talks nice to each other."

"Yeah. If you're mad, you can just walk to someplace else in the
classroom and not say anything. My dad says 'just walk away.'
You don't have to say 'shut up' or anything."

Note the process. Note the basic understandings being established. (Following discussion, these can be listed on posterboard and
displayed in a prominent place in the classroom for future reference.)

A. **Use words. Talk to each other.**
B. **If angry, wait until you can use kind words.**
C. **Separation is better than conflict.**

---

2. Cooperation Over Competition. Most of the time, one student's helping another student solve a classroom science problem is
not "cheating" or unfair. Our job is to clarify the difference. The best
way to do so is to establish cooperation as the norm. Specifically, this
means planning and carrying out cooperative learning practices in
the classroom, by having students work in pairs and in small groups
for at least half their time in school (see Slavin, 1994). From the basic
understanding that cooperation is the norm, students can then learn
that certain unusual situations (such as during a quiz or test) are
competitive times, one of those few times when sharing information
with another is not the right thing to do.

Examples: What is cheating? (limits). How does a student show
interest in helping another? (courtesies). As a seventh-grade example:

"What is the difference between helping and cheating?"
"Well, cheating is when you get caught!"
"So if you don't get caught, Alicia, it's okay to cheat?"
"No . . . I'm not sure, actually."
"Jena, you look like you're eager to speak. Go ahead."
"Cheating is when you think you are helping somebody, but you
really are hurting them."

" 'Hurting them'? How do you mean that?"

"Well, if the teacher thinks it's Jay's work, but it really isn't, it's like you're lying."

"When else do you not help someone? Andrew?"

"Um, if it's a test. You're not supposed to help somebody do their test."

"Yes. But what if you're both working together on a project? Is it okay to share answers?"

"Uh huh! If Jay is working with me on a science project, that's not cheating. We're helping each other learn."

Note the basic understandings being established:

A. **Helping others is a normal thing to do.**
B. **Sometimes we work without helping others.**
C. **It's good to help and be helped.**

---

3. Achievement Is Valued. Again, just as we need to set cooperation as the norm, so, too, is student achievement considered expected and welcome. One way we can do this is by broadening our scope of achievement. Because schools narrowly emphasize language and math to the exclusion of other areas, many teachers use Howard Gardner's (1983) multiple intelligences as a guide to encouraging, recognizing, and teaching to other talent areas ("intelligences") such as musical, kinesthetic, spatial, and interpersonal. Even more fundamental is a positive class attitude valuing achievements, regardless of the areas of achievement themselves.

Examples: Should students get special privileges because they get 100% on an exam? (limits). Is it okay to brag about your successes? Should you act kindly toward another student whom you think is uninteresting? (courtesies). As in this fourth-grade example:

"We have our four group 'winter performances' coming up soon. It's going to be important to use all the talents you have in

your group. Spend 5 minutes talking about the different jobs
and roles we've listed on this chart. Talk about who in your
group might do which jobs and roles."

"Stefan? What did your group come up with?"

"Well, Maria likes to talk—right?—so we thought she'd be a good
narrator. Philip can bring in his guitar and do music. I'm not
good at anything, so . . . "

"Nothing? Let me ask Stefan's group: What does Stefan do well?
Philip?"

"Stefan can write the script out. He always gets good marks in
writing like book reports and stuff."

Note the basic understandings being established:

A. **Different talents are important here.**
B. **Each of us excels at something.**
C. **We all value excellence.**

4. Full Inclusion Is Practiced. In a legal sense, inclusion means that
under threat of penalty to you or the school, a student must physically
be in your room and have equal access to classroom materials and fa-
cilities. In the more important prosocial sense, a classroom is more than
a collection of individuals. Inclusion in a prosocial classroom means
that students see and are inclined toward a common good—the good
of others in addition to their own individual good. They learn how to
live with one another and how to be part of a group. They learn how to
get their needs met, but not at the expense of others. Hence, inclusion
sets the foundation for the "small society" of the classroom (remember
the Netsilik?). All students belong here (and only under unusual circumstances are they absent from the classroom).

Examples: What behaviors are not helpful to the group? (limits).
How do we treat a new student to our classroom? When is it okay to
interrupt a speaker? (courtesies). Take this eighth-grade example:

"In the school I used to go to, the kids were all stuck up. If you
   didn't have the right clothes, you were nobody."

"That sounds pretty bad to me, Latricia. Is it different here?"

"Yeah, well, a little. Actually it's mostly the same in this school,
   but I think it's different here in this class if you know what I
   mean?"

"You feel comfortable in our class. Good. Does anyone feel uncomfortable? Dan?"

"No, I agree with Latricia. The kids here are like other kids—
   they're rude outside. . . . But when we're here we're not jerks
   to each other."

"Why is that?"

"Maybe . . . maybe because we have to get along being all in the
   same room? I don't know, but it's a lot easier to get along in
   here than outside!"

Note the basic understandings being established:

A. **This classroom (school) is a good place to be.**
B. **Each of us can get our needs met.**
C. **Everyone here belongs here.**

Supporting the Basic Understandings

There are several conditions that must exist for the basic understandings to become established.

First, as evidenced by the discussion dialogue in the last example,
your classroom should be a safe place. Students must feel free to speak
and act without being ridiculed or ignored. Toward this end, students
will take their cues from the teacher—how you react to students' opin-
ions and actions. For all students, safety requires limits. These should
clearly describe appropriate reactions to the ideas and words of others.

Second, there is an African proverb that states, "It takes an entire
village to raise a child." No matter what the educational level of your

classroom, use whatever resources are available in your community. Whether in the city or country, banks, retail stores, and businesses are often willing to help out—talk to students, have students participate, or even simply welcome a class visit. Parents are a key part of the "village." Talk with them about basic understandings you are seeking to establish. You don't need to require parents to "practice" at home with their children. These might be either insulting or impossible tasks for some parents. Involve them—at the very least—by talking with them about what you are working toward: prosocial behavior.

Third, model and demonstrate prosocial behavior. Children imitate what we do more than what we say, particularly when it comes to behavior. In a fascinating study of the effects of modeling on children, researchers had adults play a game with children where the children could win money (Bryan & Walbek, 1970). Nearby was a box for donations to "poor children." Each adult sat and played a game with a child. The adult also pointed out the donation box, either complaining about it or advocating donating to it. Half the adults who advocated donating actually got up and donated, and half the adults who complained about donating actually donated as well. The outcome? Children tended to follow adults' actions rather than words: Children who saw an adult donate tended to do the same, whether or not the adult spoke for or against donation, and children who saw an adult not donate did not themselves donate, even if the adult spoke for donating.

Fourth, be careful with rewards, especially material rewards. Although stickers, stars, and prizes can provide momentary fun, they send students the wrong message: Behave well because then you'll get a reward. A basic understanding, however, is that prosocial behavior is expected of all, not only those who choose to strive for a reward. As I said before, basic understandings are not options. We should never regard them—or present them to students—as choices, like picking a lunch entree. Yes, we can and should praise prosocial behavior as a model: "John, you did a great job working as a team with Sue and Jim today." "Jessie, thank you for holding the door for Gina—she had an armful of books!" "Zoe, I think it's splendid how you're helping Angela get used to our class." Never materially reward students for cooperating, for respecting others, or for taking good care of their own bodies. The difference between praising pro-social behavior and materially rewarding that behavior is subtle but very, very important. In opposing automatic and mindless reward-ing, Alfie Kohn proposed that those rewards "do not alter the atti-tudes that underlie our behaviors. They do not create an enduring commitment to a set of values or to learning; they merely, and tem-porarily, change what we do"(Kohn, 1993).

Fifth, establish basic understandings at a personal level. Basic understandings are not an abstract set of principles or rules the stu-dents "subscribe to" or "promise to uphold." As I said earlier, words alone can deceive; words can fool us into thinking children have actually learned good behavior. Besides, there is little connection be-tween what children say and what they actually do. In one early and famous study, children who cheated were just as likely to say that cheating was wrong as children who did not cheat at all (Hartshorne & May, 1930).

"Making it personal" means having each student be personally accountable for his or her actions. Talk must be geared not toward the production of rote repetition (regurgitation) but toward the outcome of personal action. Establishing basic understandings uses pronouns— "I," "our," and "me," but mostly "you": "Tell me about how someone was helpful to you this morning. What did they do that was helpful?"

Or the teacher saying: "I was pleased with how you helped our new student during computer class. You asked Ashley to sit with you and be part of your team!"

Personal accountability for the limits and courtesies that compose basic understandings are not religious, nor should they be geared toward pushing any religious agenda or perspective. Although many religions incorporate moral behavior in their belief systems, basic understandings serve to advance only one simple point of view: human survival. Human survival violates no religious belief. We will not survive as a culture (or as a nation or as a species) unless we teach our young people the limits and courtesies of basic understandings we all need to get along with each other.

In summary: Rules do not teach. Free yourself and your students from "crime-and-punishment" thinking. Instead, establish basic under-standings with your students by teaching them limits and courtesies. Students don't need rules when basic understandings are constantly being advanced by the teacher and developed by the class. Make your classroom safe for students. Model prosocial behavior in your words and actions. Talk with parents and involve others as appropriate. Treat your students like persons, not captives. Praise and give acknowledgment to students for acting human, but do not reward them for doing so. Make basic understandings stick at a personal level by actively and concretely teaching and practicing them.

II

Three Key
Dimensions of
Positive Classroom
Management

3

Setting Up a Safe and Productive Learning Environment

SCHOOLS and classrooms are artificial learning environments. Think about this: We seat a child for 6 hours in an overheated room bathed in fluorescent light, among 20 to 30 (or more) other eager, restless, or bored children, and insist that they all stay seated and/or keep quiet for long periods of time during that day!

Many teachers are working to overcome this dreary scenario through the use of, for example, more highly interactive cooperative learning approaches. Yet too many students still face each day in what can only be described as an institutional warehouse, and in some worse cases, a prison, discouraging to the spirit and destructive of any curiosity and enthusiasm to learn.

Are these adequate situations for learning? Is learning even possible under such circumstances? The answers are obvious. There is hope. It starts with you, a teacher who wants to make school a hospitable place for learning. Perhaps you have seen a teacher who accomplishes this with little things in his or her classroom: the teacher who uses children's works—art, for example—to decorate a classroom, or the teacher who makes her classroom a safe place even when streets outside are dangerous, or the teacher whose imaginative set-up of classroom furniture frees students from being anchored in a seat for hours at a time.

Teaching prosocial behavior does not occur in a vacuum. It takes place somewhere. That somewhere, that environment (typically, the classroom) is the physical dimension of positive classroom management. The physical dimension should receive your first and most basic consideration. Prior to instruction, and before you address managerial issues, think about and then act on the classroom's physical environment you and the students will occupy. Yes, there are limitations to what you can change: You can't change the building, the size of the classroom, the number of students, or the social class and family income of the students you'll have in that classroom. There is much you can (and must) influence, however, ranging from the first impression someone gets upon entering the room, to the comfort and safety experienced by the students. It takes a little thought and planning, but not much money or time.

Specifically, how can we set up the classroom to be a safe and productive learning environment? To begin, focus on these three areas: The "nuts 'n' bolts" (desks, tables, bookcases, and that stuff); the human factor (how people will use the stuff); and the ambience (feeling of the room). Perhaps as you read the following, have a pen and paper handy to make notes on your own physical environment.

First are the concrete, tangible, "nuts 'n' bolts" considerations. Each student must have a place to work and a place to store his or her things. Decide whether students will use desks or tables, and see if they are in good condition and appropriate for your students. The lighting should be strong enough to prevent eyestrain; heat should not put people to sleep, nor the lack of it allow icicles to grow on noses. How is the noise level? Is there a noisy or highly distracting condition emanating from within the school? Outside the school? There should also be no obvious safety problems, and this includes having adequate entrance and exit doorways.

Second is the human factor. How will you and the students "live together" in this rather tight (or gaping) space for most of a year? How can you set it up to maximize the educational benefit for and your students?

Essentially, students need to be able to see and hear you, and vice versa. No matter what type of classroom you run, your lines of sight and sound to all areas of the classroom must be unobstructed. In fact, you need clear lines of sight from many different parts of the classroom: the door, the teacher's desk, the chalkboard. Your students' lines of sight and sound count, too. Put yourself in their places: Are chalkboards and bulletin boards placed at their sight level? Are desks and tables the right size and height for your students?

Also essential is the idea that human beings have to move about. Will there be space for this to occur comfortably? Will people crash into one another? Potential behavior problems can be eliminated if traffic lanes are uncluttered and are as wide as possible. There will be times when students stay put. At these times, you'll want students to work in comfort, but beware of making things too comfortable lest they fall asleep! (I've seen downy sofas and plush-lined bathtubs in the classroom that can rapidly bring on slumber!)

Third is the intangible, the ambience. *Ambience* is the French word for environment or surroundings—that unnameable feeling you experience upon setting foot in a room. It comes from everything—odors, humidity, ventilation, chalk dust, heat, cold, noise, echo, and quiet. They all come together to give a room a unique ambience. Walk in as a stranger a few times when the room is still new to you. Use all your senses: What strikes you? What feels good? What needs to be changed?

Using less than $100 worth of materials, New York City fourth-grade teacher Mary Sullivan treated her classroom to a makeover, with the help of California teacher and designer Frank Garcia. The makeover included colorful new bulletin board designs, an inviting reading center and book display, and a novel art learning center. It even included a special lightweight stool so Mary no longer had to perch herself on the edge of a desk or crouch uncomfortably as she worked with her students (Murray, 1994).

Don't discount ambience. Each room has its own "feel," and that feel sends an immediate message to each person who visits for 6 minutes, or to each captive who must occupy that room for 6 hours a day. Air fresheners are inexpensive and last 3 months. Sunlight freshens dark corners. Green foliage plants clean the air. (I've heard that spider plants remove carbon monoxide.) Teachers can invite the students to contribute to the ambience of the classroom. Flowers from your students' gardens are free. (Yes, even dandelions count. They grow all over New York City, Chicago, Los Angeles, and cities and towns across the country!)

4

Teaching So Students
Stay Focused and Learn

THE instructional dimension describes how to teach so that students can stay focused and learn. It is the not-so-obvious area of classroom management. People forget that the way a teacher teaches—what he or she says and does—is an essential part of classroom management. You cannot ignore the instructional area, although that's precisely what teachers do when they buy ready-made "discipline" packages and plans. These do not work because they are unrealistic; they ignore the fact that the manner of teaching influences student behavior. Successful teachers know that teaching behaviors are more fundamental to students learning prosocial behavior than any "discipline" kit, program, plan, or package.

Which teacher behaviors result in prosocial student behavior? There are many. I have settled on five that stand out, from my personal experience as a teacher and principal, and from my reading of the professional education literature. These teacher behaviors allow students to learn, and they foster prosocial student behavior.

First, the teacher clearly communicates instructional expectations for students. California teacher Jaime Escalante, portrayed in the film *Stand and Deliver,* was horrified at the low expectations his colleagues held for their students. Escalante's high (but not unrealistic) expectations for success dramatically raised student achievement, so that a majority of his inner-city high school students were accepted into advanced placement college-level courses. It is no surprise that student behavior in his classroom also improved in response to those high academic expectations.

Second, a teacher conveys enthusiasm for the subject and for teaching that subject to students. Indeed, enthusiasm has been identified in many studies to be the most significant characteristic of an effective teacher. Teacher enthusiasm not only positively affects student behavior, it improves student achievement as well. Enthusiasm is shown in many ways: a "let's find out" attitude, use of voice, moving around the classroom, and perhaps most of all, sharing and articulating interest in the subject. Mr. Escalante was not afraid to show students he was interested in math—he shared his enthusiasm by coming up with novel and interesting approaches to common math problems. It is also important to note that he made the classroom safe for students to express their enthusiasm, too.

Third, a teacher must keep students accountable for their work. Due dates and requirements must be clear. The teacher must then proceed to hold students to those dates and requirements. Students should not be "let off the hook," because when students are held accountable for their work the quality and quantity of their work rises. Classroom misbehavior is minimal when students are productively occupied and held accountable for their work.

Fourth, a teacher must be aware of what is happening in the classroom. My dear Aunt Flora, who began teaching before the Great Depression, used to say that "A good teacher has eyes in the back of her head." Teachers must develop a sense of classroom movement based on that awareness. At times, this means "dovetailing"—doing two things at once. I saw my aunt as a principal years later, speaking to a class of sixth-graders in her New York City elementary school. As she discussed an issue with the class, I saw her approach John, who was noisily spinning a pencil on his desk. What would she do? Without pausing at all, or breaking eye contact with the class, Aunt Flora quietly solved the problem by simply touching John's desk. John immediately stopped playing with the pencil as she continued to speak to the class. I was amazed by the smooth and economical way she handled the situation!

Fifth, one must teach for student success. In addition to the previous four teaching behaviors, this fifth element has an enormous impact on producing prosocial behavior: teaching for student success. Student success is a sum of the four teacher behaviors, because teachers who convey enthusiasm, communicate expectations, keep students accountable, and are aware of what is happening in the classroom are ensuring student success. Student success—doing well in school—is connected to everything we hold dear as educators: the chance for students to get a good job, to have high self-esteem, and to be a contributing member of society.

Three Axioms for Student Success and Positive Classroom Management

Our job as teachers is to do more than hold up hoops for students to jump through, judge who passes and who fails, or merely hope our students succeed. Our job is to ensure that students succeed. But what has student success to do with classroom management?

Students who feel successful are seldom behavior problems.

All but the most hardened of teachers want their students to feel successful. Ever since the very first student flunked the very first exam, teachers have been concerned with how to help students do better in school. Some teachers try to achieve this by making school more "user friendly." They seek to be more permissive and/or cordial. Others respond by being stricter or by demanding students follow a rigid structure. Both responses miss the mark. Permissiveness and authoritarianism are extremes, and although they may help the teacher feel more agreeable or in control, they do not work toward greater success for students. What, then, really works? How can our students feel successful?

To feel successful, students must actually be successful.

Acceptance, praise, and rewards from the teacher may temporarily make a student feel good, but they do not directly translate into student success. Even getting high grades (the traditional indicator of school success) does not necessarily boost a student's sense of success. On the other hand, when a student actually experiences success, that experience creates an impression that is far more powerful than any teacher's words, grades, or rewards, but in order to experience success, the student must do something.

To actually be successful, a student must first do something of value.

Feelings of success come when a student actually does something of value—participating, performing, creating, practicing, designing, producing, carrying out an experiment, finishing an assignment, or any of hundreds of other "doing" activities. In the final analysis, what the student does will have a greater impact on how successful the student is (and feels he or she is) than what the teacher knows, says, or believes.

These three axioms are especially relevant to elementary and middle school teaching, because these are the years when children are absorbed by activity and by wanting to do something well. Anyone who has taught second-graders has seen them waving their papers, seeking the teacher's attention and approval: "Is this right?" they ask. "Is this good?" they wonder. Middle-school teachers see how sixth- and seventh-graders bristle at the meaninglessness of busy work.

Doing well in school really does matter to children, even those who pretend otherwise. Sadly, children quickly learn to label success and failure in the classroom: A kindergarten child will readily name the "good" (well-behaved) kids and the "bad" kids. At any elementary or middle-school grade, students can promptly identify the "winners" (successful kids) and the "losers" (the rest).

What can you do to address this problem? More important, what can you do that will help, without adding yet another layer of things to an already busy day? The answer is simple. By doing a few things you now do slightly differently, you can dramatically raise the level and frequency of student success in your classroom.

I have put together a list of 12 practical instructional strategies you can implement immediately in your classroom to ensure student success. As you read them, keep the three axioms in mind.

1. **Students who feel successful are seldom behavior problems.**
2. **To feel successful, students must actually be successful.**
3. **To actually be successful, a student must first do something of value.**

For each week from mid-September through December (12 weeks), or for any 12-week period in the school year, pick one of the following strategies per week. Work at it for the week. Monitor yourself each day as to how well you carried out that strategy.

Twelve Instructional Strategies

What follows are 12 practical instructional strategies teachers can use to promote student achievement and prosocial behavior:

1. First (and this is basic to all quality classroom teaching), gear your group instruction to the correct level of difficulty. Especially with new teachers, too much teaching time is spent in instruction that either is too simplistic or is beyond students' ability. Establish groups within your classroom for instruction, and try to aim your classroom

instruction at the point of just manageable difficulty—a point just slightly beyond your students' current achievement level. Try to get a sense of where they are. For example, this evening, before you put away that stack of checked/graded student work, hold that pile of papers in your hand and skim them; try to get a sense of the overall difficulty level. Was the work too easy? Too hard? Make adjustments accordingly. Yet be patient: Even the most experienced of teachers continue to be challenged in locating that point of "just manageable difficulty!"

2. Second, you make success definite when you make failure impossible. This sounds too good to be true, but it's not really that difficult. Break instruction into smaller learnings. For example, teaching students to use a computer requires they first learn how to use a mouse and/or keyboard. Be sure to teach basic keyboard orientation before lurching into programming. If you equip students with prerequisite tools, mastering the task and attaining success becomes doable.

3. Build patterning and association into each lesson. At one time, we can store only about four or five bits of new information in our minds. Let's say there are 20 new vocabulary words—in science, math, or social studies. Teach students to pattern them; divide them into four or five subgroups. They could be grouped by initial letter (hemlock, hickory, hawthorne, holly, hornbeam), by mnemonics (Argentina, Brazil, Chile), or by other patterns. Challenge older students to come up with their own patterns.

Association means connecting new concepts/learnings to what students already know. Have students build on what they already know by comparing, contrasting, or making analogies with new material. For instance, when introducing the concept of multiplication, help students discover that multiplication (unfamiliar, new concept) is really the same as old, familiar addition. The strange new multiplication algorithm 3 x 5 is nothing more than adding 5 + 5 + 5.

4. Fourth, monitor student work. Like a ship passing through locks along a canal, monitor student work as it proceeds. Establish checkpoints, especially for involved or lengthy assignments (papers, experiments, projects, presentations). At each daily or weekly checkpoint, give students evaluative comments along the way. Don't wait until the project is done. Or try this: Instead of doing all monitoring

yourself, have classroom partners check each other's work-in-progress. Provide blank checklists for students to use in evaluating their own and/or their partners' evolving projects.

5. You ensure success when you give students the most precious commodity we have: time. Avoid sound bite fragmentation! Provide adequate time for students to process—to do something with—what they have learned. Research shows us that when students process what they have learned, they not only stay focused for a longer period of time, they retain more.

How can you avoid fragmentation? When asking questions, use *wait time:* Simply wait 3 to 5 seconds after asking a question. (Many teachers wait less than 1 second after asking a question!) Wait time increases student involvement, allows richer student responses, and brings slower students into classroom instruction. Whole block scheduling (longer periods of instruction) is used in some schools to allow students more time to process what they are learning.

Speaking of time, you can ensure success by eliminating "hang loose" time. A strategy I used with success was "do now" work. As soon as students entered the classroom, I had a "do now" assignment written on the chalkboard. This eliminated instances of dawdling and getting into mischief. But with "do now" work, they wasted no time getting started. (Nonnegotiable!) Some teachers have students work on journals as soon as they enter. Others have students work in groups checking their work, or working at an activity center. Either way, "do now" work helps students become focused and more self-sufficient, and it also allows the teacher time to take attendance, collect money, and put out fires that some students bring to school within themselves.

How else can you have students process what they have learned? Have them teach! If children and teens are asked to teach someone else something they know, that is an incredibly powerful way for students to process what they have learned. Rotate assignments to make sure each student gets an opportunity to teach.

6. Make "successful" mean fruitful and productive, not victorious. In hockey or football, when one team wins, the other must lose, but classrooms are no place for that I-win-so-you-lose rule. Assign as many A's as you honestly can when student work has met the criteria. The criteria should never be the number of others who did well.

Robert Slavin of Johns Hopkins University has written extensively and persuasively about the value of cooperative learning, where students work together in heterogeneous (mixed ability) teams to master material presented by the teacher. Moreover, cooperative learning directly contributes to positive classroom management. Slavin acknowledges that "most cooperative learning classrooms are well behaved, because students are motivated to learn and are actively engaged in learning activities" (Slavin, 1990, p. 115).

Evaluate more but judge less. Avoid making unnecessary good-bad, pass-fail achievement distinctions. For example, such distinctions are especially inappropriate for cooperative writing projects, poetry reading, science exhibits, constructing a computer database, community action projects, political polling, sculpting, and hundreds of other endeavors. Sometimes we teachers spend more time judging than teaching. French essayist Joseph Joubert (1928) said that "children need models rather than critics."

7. You can ensure success when you get to know your students' other strengths. It will open up new areas for them to demonstrate successful learning. Start with getting to know their likes and dislikes. What are they good at? Have older students complete an interest inventory. Ask young students to name things they do well outside of school.

Consider using Howard Gardner's (1983) theory of multiple intelligences as a guide to teaching to a wider variety of student abilities. Gardner highlights seven areas or "intelligences," namely, linguistic, logical-mathematical, spatial, musical, bodily-kinesthetic, interpersonal, and intrapersonal intelligences. Schools have traditionally emphasized the first two (linguistic and logical-mathematical) intelligences. Recognizing the other five opens new areas for student success: drawing, organizing, synthesizing, building, rebuilding, designing, predicting, and hundreds of others. [For excellent applications of Gardner's theory, see Thomas Armstrong's (1994) *Multiple Intelligences in the Classroom*.] One of my fifth-grade students struggled for years with reading. In her first school Mary had been—in her mother's words—"remediated to death." By talking with Mom, we learned that Mary had a talent for photography. She had a shoe box of stunning close-up color photographs she had taken of flowers. What an exhibit Mary presented at that year's PTA carnival!

8. Perhaps most important of all, teach students to take responsibility for their learning. Nothing will certify you as an excellent teacher more than your teaching students to be in charge of their own work. We often hear talk about being an independent learner, but few know how to help students do so. Most teachers make students too dependent upon the teacher. As a result many students define success in school simply as an ability to follow directions and repeat back to the teacher what the student thinks the teacher values. Although following directions is a skill in convergent tasks (some types of problem solving), too much of it can stand in the way of a student taking responsibility for his or her learning.

Teachers can also empower students by involving them more fully in what they are learning. When I taught music in a Brooklyn elementary school, I made up a simple songsheet for my fourth-grade song-flute students. I handed it to the office for duplication, but it came back in my mailbox with a "see me" note from the principal. "What was wrong with my songsheet?" I asked. He told me "You're doing too much for your students! Do your students know how to write a G-clef?" he asked. "No," I admitted. "Do they know how to write music notes yet?" "No, not yet." "Then give them blank staff paper and have them write the notes and musical symbols! Teach them!" he urged.

He was right on target. Years later, as a principal myself, I repeated that same message to my teachers: "If you do too much for students, you rob students of the chance to do for themselves." In its extreme, it can turn children into educational invalids. Helplessness is a vicious circle; children who see themselves as victims will act accordingly.

Involve the students in decisions that affect their school day. As you teach, try to get comfortable talking to your students as a group, and talk in a way that involves them in planning their day. For example, once morning got started, I would give my students an overview of the day ahead. Some activities were not negotiable (opening exercises, testing, lunch, etc.), but others were flexible: "I'm thinking of spending more time on math this morning to give you more time to work on those fraction problems we began yesterday. That means our (puppet show) will come after lunch. Does that sound good?" I'd ask the students, and I'd be prepared to go with their thoughts if sound reasons were provided.

Contracting is one technique to help older elementary and middle-school students take responsibility for their learning. The student and/ or teacher draw up a contract, which spells out requirements and time for completion, and the contract is signed by student and teacher.

9. Students will be more successful when they are interested. Perhaps no strategy is more obvious—yet is as frequently ignored—than this one. All of us will do something more readily if we are interested in what we are doing. Educators have known for years that students who are interested in what they are doing will not only enjoy doing it but will do the activity for a longer period of time. They will learn more from the activity. Our job is to increase student interest.

What can you as a teacher do to increase student interest? Two things. First, vary your instructional methods. Instead of relying on one style of teaching ("chalk and talk" lecture, for example), involve students in a task where they can "go hands-on." Or demonstrate something. Or use simulation games. Or hold a guided class discussion. Students who are not adept at speaking in class are usually first to join in when an interesting class discussion begins. Similarly, students who are reticent about writing may be transformed when allowed to write, for instance, using a computer.

Another way to increase student interest is to teach in "multiple modalities." Between 70% and 90% of classroom time is devoted to verbal activities: lecturing, reading from a text, writing, and so forth. Ironically, words and numerals are highly abstract and harder to assimilate, especially for young children and slower learners. They also quickly lead to boredom. Instead of a blizzard of words, provide demonstrations, pictures, visual-spatial, and multisensory activities that utilize concrete and pictorial modalities. These latter two modalities are best for learners who have little prior knowledge of the idea or topic. Using pictures is better than using words, but the concrete—the real thing—is best of all. The pictorial mode works when concrete is not possible or practicable. The use of abstractions (words and numerals) is more suitable when learners already have some prior understanding. Abstractions—no matter how colorful the words—cannot promote student understanding the way concrete objects can.

Along the same lines, novelty and variety in classroom instruction can renew interest, but beware: Too much of novelty or variety in a short period of time makes students passive observers. (Television produces passivity precisely because it consists of novel, rapidly changing images where the viewer remains just a viewer and never a "doer.") In the classroom, too much novelty becomes entertainment, and it moves the focus from the learner to the performer (teacher). Variety is fine, but providing students with too many choices can be counterproductive, setting up unrealistic expectations about the nature and reality of the world of work and adult social interaction. In addition, providing too many choices causes students to lose focus and, ultimately, to lose interest.

10. Provide evaluation that is realistic and feedback that is immediate and detailed. Realistic evaluation helps students connect what they have learned with the real world. For example, a multiple-choice test on the solar system is not as realistic (or helpful to the student) as building a small model of the solar system. That model would be a more authentic test than a multiple-choice test because the model is more closely related to the real thing.

Feedback from the teacher is an important type of evaluation. To be effective, feedback must be immediate (right away) and detailed (explicit). Immediate means grading and returning students' exams or papers as soon as possible. Detailed means making your evaluation remarks more than a number or letter grade, describing what was done well and what did not meet the requirements. Saying "Super!" or "Good work" is not as helpful to a learner as "I'm glad you remembered to reduce these fractions to lowest terms!" or "See how much more legible your handwriting is today compared to this paper you did in September!"

Keep in mind that praise is a type of feedback that can work wonders. To work best, praise should be authentic and specific, and never given out of pity or used excessively.

11. Learn to ask—and practice asking—good questions. Benjamin Bloom (1980) called questioning an "alterable variable," meaning that it is a skill that teachers can learn and can improve in.

There are questions that go nowhere: "What is the capital of Oklahoma?" Then there are questions that produce thinking: "Can you say that differently?" "Predict what the vacuum cleaner dust will look like under the microscope." "In what ways are deserts alike?"

When questioning the entire class, ask broad, open-ended questions instead of yes/no, one-right-answer questions. Probe for meaning and encourage other students to build on initial student responses. A good technique to use is "alerting," where you first pose a question to the entire group, then select one student to respond. Teachers violate this by saying "Tom, what is the largest country in Asia?" As a result only Tom will attend. Instead, announce: "I'm going to call on someone at the end of this question, so be ready!"

What is the best way for teachers to answer or respond to student questions? Psychologist David Elkind (1987, pp. 119-124) advises parents and teachers to respond at the child's "level of purpose." For instance, if a 4-year-old asks why the sun shines, would it be appropriate to describe the sun's shining as "a result of an incandescent ball of gases undergoing rapid thermonuclear fusion?" Instead, the child's level of purpose is himself, and he sees the sun shining in that context: "The sun shines so I can play outside." When you respond to students' questions, do not overfill the "cup of curiosity." Do not feel you must have all the answers. Leaving a student with questions is more valuable than providing answers. Besides, the best questions are those that you cannot readily answer, and the same is true for your students.

What about your "body English" as you respond to questions? Do you appear interested in students' responses? Bored? Impatient? Try setting up a mirror on the back wall of the classroom opposite from where you usually stand in addressing the class. Glance at your reflection as you ask questions. Or arrange for someone to videotape you while teaching. When I forced myself to see myself as the students saw me, I was at first very uncomfortable and self-conscious, but that mirror ultimately helped me to adjust my pace in asking questions, and it also confirmed for me what I was doing well.

12. Work toward smooth flow and lively pacing. Strive for smoothness, and avoid breaking the flow of instruction. Sometimes teachers make mountains out of molehills by pointing to a paper on the floor and announcing: "THIS ROOM IS A MESS! I AM TIRED OF SEEING PAPER ON THE FLOOR!" This just disturbs the class and gets them unfocused from their work. In extreme, it makes you an entertainer who is not very entertaining. Interruptions from bells, from the office,

and from student misbehavior all destroy flow. You cannot do much about the bells, but students are another matter: Do not reprimand or even look at a student who is seeking to interrupt as you are teaching: Hold out your hand ("stop") or an index finger ("one minute") to the interrupter, without taking your attention from the student who is talking to you. Try to follow through on your sentences, and when you are giving instructions, have students wait until you are finished before you field their questions.

New teachers tend to have a problem with pacing, either dragging or going too fast. Both extremes cause problems: Too fast = confusing; confusion = boredom; boredom = misbehavior. Too slow is just as bad: dragging = boredom; boredom = misbehavior.

Appropriate pacing is achieved by being sensitive to the "pulse" of the class, then moving at a pace ever so slightly faster than that pulse (like a surfer, perhaps, riding the crest of a wave). Probably the best technique to help you travel at the right pace in instruction is to ask questions as you teach. Student responses to your questions will give you an accurate "pulse count" of the group. Questions also allow a "time out" as you teach: Look around and sense if you're losing some of the class to boredom and should be moving on.

In addition, questions not only give you feedback, they also cause students to do something. "How are plants and molds alike?" can cause students to think, but "Brainstorm and write down five ways that plants and molds are alike" will cause them to think and to do something productive, and will keep the pace lively. By asking them to do something, you have instantly involved the student in learning and banished boredom.

Tip: In most activities like this brainstorm, don't wait for all or even most of your students to be finished before you move on. By the time that happens, the ones who were finished first are bored, and perhaps acting out. Move your eyes over the class, and when about half the class (and no more!) have finished, tell the entire group to finish up what they're working on. Then move on without waiting. Have them then share their brainstorms with a partner (this will allow those who weren't done to catch up without having the whole group wait). Again, keep things moving. Even set a time limit for sharing:"I'm going to give you 3 minutes to share brainstorms. Ready? Start!"

Keep to your word—you don't necessarily have to call time at exactly 3 minutes to the nanosecond, but when you do call time, mean it. Don't give in to "I'm not done!" protests. Provide those students with the chance to find time later on to finish.

As you have students report on their brainstorms and sharing, start one group reporting to the class. You don't need to formally say "OKAY. EVERYONE QUIET. JOHN'S GROUP IS ABOUT TO . . . SHIRLEY, I'M WAITING!" and so forth. No, you don't need to demand perfect silence before proceeding: Once they hear a group reporting they will quiet down. This means you do not have to make your words the only focal point at every classroom transition!

Look back over the list of 12 strategies.

Pick one strategy and work at it for one week.

If you have a mentor, a buddy teacher, or another trusted colleague, ask him or her to observe your teaching and help monitor your progress toward mastery of those strategies that you need to address.

5

Managing a Smooth-Running Classroom

FOR many teachers, the managerial dimension is synonymous with classroom management itself. Indeed, it does consist of planning for all the noninstructional routines that are so important to a smooth-running classroom. In addition, the term *managerial* describes another significant area: what to do about student behavior. This includes questions such as: How will the teacher plan —lay the groundwork—for prosocial student behavior? How will the teacher support prosocial behavior? How will the teacher help students "keep it up"? And the ultimate question: What should the teacher do in response to misbehavior? How can teachers correct antisocial student behavior?

In response, teachers ought to approach this managerial dimension from three perspectives: preventing, or what to do before the fact of misbehavior; supporting, or the modeling and maintaining of prosocial student behavior; and (in answer to the ultimate question), correcting, or what to do after the fact, once misbehavior has occurred. Keep in mind that although teachers historically have been most interested in ways to correct student behavior, preventing and supporting prosocial behavior are far more effective managerial tools to use in setting up a prosocial classroom.

Read through the following section to gain an understanding of each perspective. To guide you further once you have read each section, I have provided step-by-step checklists for you to use in each area.

Preventive Measures: Before the Fact

From a preventive viewpoint, the teacher must first get on top of the situation. Early on, she or he should start thinking about basic school procedures, for instance, the school's policies. What are they? What do they hold you to do? In today's world of concern over drug abuse, child abuse, and AIDS, school districts have specific policies related to each of these (and many more) issues. You should be familiar with your school's policies. This includes policies about school trips, emergencies, fire drills, and arrival and dismissal.

At the classroom level, prevention means laying the groundwork. Even before you meet them, get to know who your students are. Read over the permanent records of your students. There should be a folder for each child in your class. Skim the records and look for "special needs" students. Learn what accommodations will be needed for these students. Find out about custody arrangements by parents who are divorced or unmarried. Get information on any behavior problems and antisocial behavior students have shown in the past. Look at the positive, too: Which students will be helpful peer models of prosocial behavior for other students? Think about some of the classroom procedures you want to institute. What will your students do each day (aside from their learning activities)? What will you do to help your students feel safe in your room? How about psychological safety? What can you do to set groundwork to support prosocial behavior by students? Are you prepared to face students who may openly mock or challenge prosocial behavior?

Generally, preventing means making decisions ahead of time on the nitty-gritty issues like school movement: whole classroom (lunch, recess, special periods); within the classroom (by groups and by individuals); and to and from the classroom (rest room, office, etc.). There are many factors to consider in the preventive side of classroom management. The checklists in Part III provide comprehensive lists of specific preventive actions teachers can take.

Supportive Measures: During the Fact

Preventive measures include supporting good behavior, too. Earlier, we discussed how teachers need to provide support for instruction by monitoring student work as it progresses. In the managerial dimension, that support is similar: Teachers work with students to carry through on the basic understandings (limits and courtesies). Supportive means having students practice prosocial behavior and includes the teacher modeling and actively lending assistance to help the students achieve those valuable prosocial behaviors.

Teachers should provide students with ongoing support. Elementary, middle-school, and high school students need more than simply to be told what to do—they need help achieving success. Take the idea of reminding students. Teachers do a disservice when they tell young students "I want to treat you like adults, so I'm not going to remind you" about a deadline pertaining to an assignment. Students are not adults, but they are—as we are—human, and we all do need to be reminded on occasion. (Would you remember to renew your driver's license without a reminder from the state motor vehicles department?) We teachers cannot assume that because we said something once, it has become ingrained. Reminding students does not mean we take on their obligation to hand in their assignment, but it does mean that we face up to our responsibility to support their desire to be successful—actually be successful—in school (DiGiulio, 1978).

Corrective Measures: After the Fact

No matter how supportive you are, and no matter how well you have taken preventive steps beforehand, there will be times students will need corrective action—action by the teacher after misbehavior has occurred. Even the best of teachers have students who at times act in antisocial ways; that is, they misbehave. When that happens, what will you do in response to that misbehavior? What do experienced teachers do?

What I'd like to do first is describe a broad approach to reacting to student misbehavior; then I'll move to specific strategies teachers can use. Teachers who are positive classroom managers share four beliefs that guide their responses to misconduct—what they do when faced with student misbehavior. I call them the four "C.E.D.E." beliefs:

Continue. They keep the teaching-learning process going. They do not involve other students, do not draw things to a halt, and do not distract uninvolved students from their tasks.

Efficiency. They identify and deal with misbehavior easily. This means they do not spend class time or student attention locating culprits, seeking witnesses, or making a mountain out of a molehill.

Dignity. They maintain dignity—theirs and the students'. They never compromise a student's dignity, even if openly insulted or challenged. They know that teacher sarcasm always makes matters worse.

Economy. They deal with misbehavior as swiftly as possible and avoid making "an example" of someone or some misbehavior. They avoid "providing free entertainment" for the class.

Taken together, these principles tell us that when a response to misbehavior is called for, skilled teachers use a stepladder of least intervention. Think of the ladder as representing a scale of teacher intensity in responding to misbehavior, with the lowest rungs the milder responses and the highest rungs the stronger responses. Just as you always start climbing a stepladder at the lowest rung, respond to student misbehavior—intervene—at the lowest possible level of intensity. Doctors should not perform surgery or prescribe drugs if bed rest is all that is needed to restore health. Similarly, if just a glance can settle a student's minor misbehavior, it is excessive (and damaging and exhausting) to publicly yell out the student's name or otherwise punish him or her.

Not every student misbehavior merits a teacher's response. Of all interventions the lowest level is nonintervention—ignoring misbehavior. Ignoring misbehavior is not, technically speaking, an intervention. Nonetheless, nonintervention—doing nothing in response to student (mis)behavior—is a valuable strategy for a teacher to use at an appropriate time. For example, misbehaviors that do not involve safety or distract other students (such as tapping a pencil eraser on the desk or staring into space for a few moments) are likely best ignored. However, never ignore student misbehavior simply because you do not know what to do about it!

My stepladder of teacher interventions includes nonverbal, humor, verbal, and physical interventions.

Nonverbal Interventions

The first (lowest) rung of the ladder is the tacit intervention of simple eye contact. At the next rung—signal interventions—the teacher makes eye contact with the student, and having secured the student's attention uses a gesture such as pointing, shaking his head, or frowning. My favorite is holding my index finger vertically and waving it back and forth ("No!") or pointing down ("Get to work!"). Be sure it is private (between yourself and student) and not public (for the entire class to see).

Closeness interventions are a step higher than eye contact and gestures. Move near the misbehaving student without drawing attention from other students. This is an especially helpful strategy when you cannot get the student's attention, as when you are waiting for eye contact that doesn't come.

Signal and closeness interventions are best. They're best because they are private, seen only by the one or two students for whom intended. Furthermore, they are not disruptive to the class, they are efficient, they preserve student dignity, they enhance your dignity, and they are economical, accomplishing much with little teacher exertion. Aim for these and you will not go home exhausted each night!

Humor Interventions

Stuck somewhere between nonverbal and verbal interventions are what I call "humor interventions." These are a special type of intervention by the teacher. Humor interventions must be used with care, yet they can be very helpful. A simple smile or humorous comment can defuse a potential trouble situation as well as help you lay groundwork for defusing future problems. Tony was reported to be "a behavior problem" in another class and was transferred to mine. I placed his desk next to my desk. ("Therapeutic relocation" I called it.) He'd notice whenever the principal came by to give me my paycheck.

With a twinkle in his eye, Tony asked me, "Payday, Mr. D?" I smiled and put it away. Later, when Tony was off-task, trying to bother another student across the classroom, I walked by his desk, pointed to his seatwork paper, and whispered, "Someday it's gonna be your payday!" I added, "and remember, Mr. D gets half, right?" This light humor helped Tony go back to his work without having me reprimand him. "Payday" became our code word for "Get back to work, Tony!"

Public humor helps, too, with the entire class, especially when it can open up discussion. Some students in my class had witnessed the tail end of a fistfight at the other end of the school yard. After the bloodied boys passed my open classroom door on their way to being escorted to the principal's office, I shook my head and said to my students, "If you're going to box, at least get paid for it!" Julio added, "Yeah, and make sure you got Blue Cross, man!" The students and I laughed, and it served as a springboard for a class discussion. Instead of moralizing about the evils of fighting, and instead of condoning fighting as a way of resolving differences, I made my point using irony, which resulted in discussion and a teachable moment for my class.

As I recall the rest of the dialogue:

"The real problem, Mr. D, is the other kids. They egg you on."
"Yeah. I got into a fight last week with Hector, and I didn't want
    to fight him, but everybody was making me."
" 'Making you'? Can somebody 'make you' fight?"
"Easy. They make you feel small if you don't. They call you 'chicken.' "
"What can you do if you don't want to fight? Jenny?"
"You can stay away from bad kids. . . ."
"You can stay away from Hector!"
"Mr. D, do you know what else you can do? Don't let other kids
    fight!"
"What do you mean by that, David?"
"You know, when you're in the circle around the kids who want
    to fight, don't let them make the kids fight who are going to
    fight."
"Isn't that hard to do?"
"Yes. No. You just tell them to back off. And if that doesn't work
    you move between the two kids. Kids really don't want to

fight. But they just don't want to look cheap by backing off. If you help them, there won't be a fight."

"That sounds good to me. What else can you do? Marc?"

Sarcasm and ridicule have no place in the classroom, and they should not be confused with genuine humor. Another caution: Humor interventions must not be used in dangerous situations, nor in ones that threaten to get out of hand. In such situations humor can send the wrong message to a student. At the right moment and time, however, humor interventions can be an extremely valuable positive classroom management tool by getting a message across while preserving human dignity.

Verbal Interventions

Verbal interventions are a higher level of intervention than private nonverbal interventions. They are typically used for students who do not respond to nonverbal interventions. Verbal interventions are also used when you must intervene more quickly and/or forcefully, such as when misbehavior is disruptive to other students. Do not use humor in these situations. To be effective, verbal interventions must be as unambiguous as possible.

At the lowest level of verbal intervention, the teacher speaks privately, directly to the student but out of earshot of anyone else. It can be a whisper ("John, this needs to be completed!") combined with a gesture. It can be a private conference at the student's or teacher's desk. Speak softly—so it does not involve others—but firmly. Be sure the child is listening, even if he or she is looking down. Do not speak if the child is fooling with another or is attending to a toy or other distraction. Unless large numbers of other students are involved, be patient. Say privately but clearly, "I'll wait for you to put down the toy so you can hear what I'm saying." Then remind the child of the standard expected in the classroom.

The next higher level of verbal intervention is public and directed at an individual. It is spoken loud enough for most or all others to hear. Many teachers erroneously start off at this level, even for misbehavior that would be best handled at a lower level. "RACHEL—IT IS ALWAYS SUCH A MESS BY YOUR DESK. PICK UP THOSE

PAPERS NOW!" What the teacher has done is waste his energy and attack Rachel's dignity, even if she gamely smiles to those around her. Worst of all, the teacher has too quickly upped the ante. By going public, this leaves little maneuvering room for more serious misbehaviors. Instead, had he simply gotten Rachel's attention while the class did their work, he could have simply pointed at the paper on the floor, and silently mouthed the word "Please" or "pa-per." I have used this with the most challenging students. It works. If you must make public verbal interventions, make them as clear and as businesslike as possible.

Verbal interventions that are public and directed to the entire class consist of a teacher addressing the entire class. Because this is what a teacher normally does in the act of teaching, great care must be taken as to the voice used. Screaming is never effective. Addressing the entire class in a serious, calm voice can help convey your dissatisfaction, for example, with a high classroom noise level. It is in these very cases that prevention works better than intervention: Doing something before the fact of group misbehavior is far more effective than trying to intervene after the fact. In the case of a high noise level, the teacher's intervention is best expressed as a prevention. In a calm, serious voice (and with all eyes on her), the teacher intervenes: "The noise level is high. Remember our discussion about how a lot of noise makes it hard to think? Let's give it another try."

Save your public voice for teaching, and use it more for prevention than for intervention.

Physical Interventions

Never touch a student. Well, almost never. Tapping a student on the shoulder or shaking a student's hand or holding a young child's hand may be acceptable. Avoid any greater physical contact (hugging, picking up kids, "horsey rides," etc.). This is true for all teachers, especially for male teachers. (Generally, the public is more uneasy about expressions of physical affection by male teachers than female teachers.) Teachers are "at risk" of being accused of child abuse if an innocent hug is misconstrued. Noncontact is a good rule of thumb for all teachers. Elementary students are young and incapable of knowing what they are getting into when receiving affectionate physical contact from an unrelated adult. In general, it's safest for all teachers—male or female—to avoid all but the most superficial of physical contacts with students.

Teachers must also avoid nonaffectionate physical contact. Corporal punishment serves no constructive purpose. It only makes matters worse. It teaches the wrong thing. It teaches that aggression should be met with aggression. Many states have laws against corporal punishment. Regardless of the existence or nonexistence of laws, never strike a child, no matter how horrid the child's behavior. After 25 years as an educator and 20 as a parent, I have never seen or heard of one beneficial outcome resulting from a teacher or parent hitting a child even when it's "for the child's good." It never is.

Crisis Time: Reacting to More Serious Problem Behaviors

As with anything else in teaching, it pays to plan ahead to when you may be faced with serious student misbehavior. Talk with teachers from past years. Ask them what worked with Sara; what did not work with Jason. Ahead of time, plan how you will react to misbehavior. What action will you take? What consequences will be carried out?

Here are several useful prosocial strategies I have collected from experienced teachers who have been faced with relatively serious student misbehavior. I have used many of these strategies myself with good results.

✓ Talking to the student: Use "I-messages": "I am disappointed by (specify student's misbehavior). I cannot allow it to continue." This is the "next step" when a student's misbehavior has not responded to supportive strategies (see above). Also, these are useful when the student can—will be allowed to and be able to—return to his work.

✘ DO NOT USE: When the student is enraged, or is likely to openly shrug off or otherwise reject your verbal disapproval.

✔ Losing classroom privileges (special events, free time or recess time, desirable tasks). This is useful when the student already knows (through class discussion) the limits and what the result or consequence of disregarding that limit must be. Limits are boundaries, and they must be clear, concise, and concrete. As discussed earlier, we teach limits best by discussion, by talking to and with our students. When the limit is disregarded and the student has gotten a supportive reminder that has not worked, the result of that violation—the consequence—means loss of a classroom privilege.

✘ DO NOT USE: If the consequence of limit violation has not been discussed by and made clear to the entire class. Do not use it as a punishment or weapon. If you do, you're likely to incur a hostile response: "I didn't want to go to recess anyway!"

✔ Exclusion from class is another consequence. It is a powerful consequence, especially in a prosocial classroom. Used sparingly, it can be very effective. However, exclusion can cause resentment, and excluding a student removes an opportunity he or she may have to learn suitable classroom behavior. As with all consequences, students must know (through prior class discussion on basic understandings and limits) the limit that was disregarded, the amount of time to be spent in exclusion, and what they are expected to do during that time.

✘ DO NOT USE: As above, if the student has not had a chance to be part of the class discussion, or he sees exclusion as a reward, or if there is not a safe, secure, and supervised place for him to spend his exile.

✔ Reflective activities. For example, writing about his misbehavior. Useful for students who are in older elementary grades and middle school. These involve self-monitoring, and are among the best noncoercive tools a teacher can use to promote self-discipline.

✘ DO NOT USE: With young children.

✓ Prosocial detention. Detention (staying after school) can be a really positive learning experience if it gives a student one-to-one time with the teacher. During this time, students can open up and let go of defensiveness (and cheekiness) that they display in front of an audience. Lunchtime is another possible time for this. A detention in which a student is isolated and sits out an hour or two is not productive; it's a waste of time and sows deep seeds of resentment.

✗ DO NOT USE: Without prior discussion of basic understandings and limits. Do not use without clear communication with the student's parent beforehand. Be clear on how and when the student will get home from school.

✓ Parental involvement is even more than important; it's necessary. Even if you do not expect there's much the parents can do to remedy their child's misbehavior, their awareness of the problem and their wish to cooperate are vital to your management plan. Involve parents early, and be prepared to outline your ideas. They will look to you for specific action, because they probably know all too well about their child's misbehavior.

✗ DO NOT USE: Generally, there is no circumstance when parental involvement is to be avoided. Caution is necessary with parents who may abuse their children in reaction to your words. Never ask parents to punish children for school misbehavior.

✓ Daily report card. This is helpful for chronic or recurring misbehavior. It offers feedback, promotes reflection, and, when used appropriately, encourages self-monitoring of behavior by the student. Draw rows and columns on a piece of paper. Each day, send it home with your signature to the right of the day's date box. In the next box to the right, write briefly how well the student did at the behavior you're focusing on. The next box to the right is for the student's signature, and the last box is for the parent's signature. Have the student initial it, take it home, and bring it back the next morning with the parent's signature. Do this for a limited time; perhaps one week to ten days is sufficient. If you wish, add another column for "parent's comments."

✗ DO NOT USE: Again, there are few circumstances when parental involvement is to be avoided. Be sure you communicate with the parent before beginning the daily report card.

✓ Self-instruction strategies have been used with success by many teachers. These strategies have students use a specific, planned-in-advance response when faced with the situation that seems to accompany misbehavior. Typically, students use self-instruction strategies as substitutes for their unacceptable behaviors. For example, a student who has thrown food in the lunchroom (at the instigation of other students) would be taught a specific strategy to use at the time of instigation. It could be as simple as getting up to use the bathroom or telling the instigators, "I'm too hungry right now" or "I don't have to do what you say." Self-instruction strategies are useful with both older and younger students.

✗ DO NOT USE: self-instruction strategies with students who have little or no insight into their own behavior. Talk to the student first; get an idea of how much insight he or she possesses.

✓ For older students, contracts can be effective. They can be used for a variety of behaviors ranging from class participation (waiting for turn to speak, raising hand) to academic production (turning in work, completing homework). Teacher and student (and sometimes parent as well) make up a contract. It should be as specific as possible, stating acceptable behavior and what credit the student will earn or get as a result of these behaviors. The contract should have a time limit—if it's too long (weeks and months) some students will have difficulty seeing it through. Make the time just long enough to allow the student to be successful in the new behavior.

✗ DO NOT USE: to negotiate basic understandings or compromise limits or courtesies. Beware of such contracts as "If I don't hit nobody for a week, I get no homework, okay?" Not hitting others is a nonnegotiable standard of behavior among human beings.

✔ Involving the principal is important for very serious misbe-havior. She or he is an important support person and should be apprised of these instances of misbehavior. Although the principal should be apprised early on of misbehavior, avoid using the principal as an enforcer.

✘ DO NOT USE: the principal's office routinely, or for anything less than very serious disturbances. This is because your leadership will be compromised (undermined) if you rely on the principal (or anyone else) to handle your classroom management.

Tougher stuff: You may be faced with the necessity to address the "tougher stuff." At these times, the main idea is to act with your head, not your emotions. Taking these situations personally removes your-self as the only rational, "cool head" present. Keep cool, calm, and collected.

✔ Dealing with fighting. The highest level of physical interven-tion is breaking up a fight, or defending yourself or another student from a student's physical attack. With regard to break-ing up a fight, if your voice does not separate the fighters, stepping between them may be the only choice you have to prevent student injury. Beware of physically intervening if you are physically smaller or weaker. In that case, send for help, and continue to use your voice—strong and clear without screaming—directed at the fighters. If you are yourself the ob-ject of attack, you certainly have the right to protect yourself. However, do so without excessive force, such as angrily pum-meling a student into submission. In anticipation of situations such as these, it's best to set up a plan with a nearby colleague for him or her to come to your assistance. As part of this plan, you might designate a trusted, reliable student to automat-ically approach Mr. Smith next door (or the principal) if you are incapacitated or otherwise involved.

✔ Dealing with threats of assault. If threatened by a student with a gun, knife, or other weapon, do not attempt to physi-cally remove the weapon. Nor should you attempt to over-power the student or direct another student to intervene. Use your voice—again, strong and clear without screaming—and clearly tell him what you're asking him to do. Go slowly. Do not make threats. Repeat your verbal directions. Be a "broken record."

Be clear that you actually are being threatened with assault. (Hearing a rumor that a child may have a knife or a gun means you should act, but it does not necessarily mean you act as if under siege or assault.) If you hear that a student has a weapon (or even if you see the outline of what looks like a weapon in a student's clothing), do not challenge the child or rush to demand immediate surrender of the weapon. Keep the student within sight while you calmly—but immediately—send for help from the principal, a counselor, or some other designated administrator.

It is a good idea to set up a plan before such an incident happens. Some schools have established a procedure for the office (principal, assistant principal, dean of students, etc.) or police to be summoned expeditiously and efficiently, and without enraging an armed and/or threatening student. If you are in an elementary or middle school and there is no plan in place, bring this subject up at a staff meeting. With your colleagues, establish a crisis intervention plan. Some schools include intervention under the term "postvention"—how the school staff will react to an unexpected, difficult incident. Check the school district's policy manual, and talk to experienced staff and administration to learn if postvention procedures are already established and, if so, what they are. A helpful reference for handling student violence and fighting is presented in Wolfgang (1995, chap. 11).

In conclusion, if you are faced with serious misbehavior that is more than disruptive and potentially harmful:

✓ Never attempt to impose consequences upon a student who is armed or a student who is distraught, visibly angry, or "fresh from the fray." Wait until the student has calmed down, even if hours are needed.

✓ Never strike a student. Even if you are openly challenged ("Go ahead, hit me!"), you will not solve a thing by hitting students. You will not lose face by refusing the student's challenge to fight, because keeping a cool head is the test of an effective classroom manager. "I don't need to hit you, John" says more about your character and professionalism than giving in. Corporal punishment is a dead end, illegal in many states. Once you resort to it, you would have to keep using it over the course of the school year to achieve compliance. You can never elicit prosocial behavior from your students if you model antisocial behavior toward them.

✓ Never attempt to use words alone when an unarmed student is out of control and likely to harm himself, herself, or another. In these most serious of cases, physically restrain and/or remove the student from the classroom. Do not strike or hurt a student in the process of restraining or removal. Reassure the student that you will not hurt him or her and that you will not allow the student to hurt you. If you are overmatched in size or bulk or both, get help immediately from another adult.

It pays to repeat: Knowing what to do before it happens helps. Even the best and most skillful teacher reactions are never as effective as teacher actions. Preventing and supporting before the fact are much better than reacting and correcting after the fact.

III

Blueprints
for Success

6

Preparing Your Classroom

ALTHOUGH we've all seen good teaching, few of us have seen the preparation that goes into it. Teachers are good because they work at it, not only as they are teaching, but in the time they spend before they walk into the classroom. Good teachers know that being prepared is essential: "Winging it" doesn't work, and it cheats students. Instructional time is wasted when a teacher flounders around trying to decide what to do next.

Because we so seldom see behind what a teacher does—teaching—I have prepared this blueprint to give an x-ray view of the work that good teachers must do in order to be successful. As a blueprint, it is not a complete representation of the finished product, but a checklist of the most basic tasks involved in preparing to teach. Tasks relate to physical setup, instruction, and managerial duties of the teacher.

There are three resources or checklists that follow, one each for early, later, and first day preparation. Early preparation tasks are those best begun at least a month or so before instruction (perhaps over summer or winter vacation break); later preparation tasks are to be attended to at least a week or two before beginning instruction. The third and final checklist is for the first day. Look over that checklist a couple of days before the first day. Bring it to school the first day as a reminder.

A few tasks in early preparation (Checklist I) may seem obvious to the more experienced teacher, but many could be easily overlooked. For instance, even the most experienced of teachers must be familiar with school policies that relate to student health and safety. For every teacher, old or new, the guiding principle for all preparation tasks is to set up a safe, healthy, educationally sound environment and program for students—a situation in which prosocial student behavior will result.

In the checklists below, review each task area and check the thumbs-up "all set" box (👍) on the left as you do so. For many, there is no one right answer. Check the box when you have taken care of the task and decided what to do about it. Check it if it does not apply so you will see at a glance the items still needing your attention.

Check the "not yet" box (✋) next to all tasks that need follow-up, task areas you are not yet clear about, or task areas that need to be taken care of before school starts. Although this first checklist should be reviewed (optimally) a month or so prior to the start of school, experienced teachers can use it midstream to double-check those things that might have been overlooked. A "Notes" section is provided at the end of each checklist where you can record items that require follow-up.

CHECKLIST I: PREPARATION—
A MONTH BEFORE INSTRUCTION

Physical
Basic classroom/school inspection:

☐ ☐ Visit the school. Bring pen and paper. Introduce yourself to the school secretary, the principal, and the school's custodian. These people will be very important to your success as a teacher.

☐ ☐ Get keys—to the school, to your classroom, and to any closets and file cabinets.

☐ ☐ Go to your classroom or teaching area. Try the keys to the classroom door, closets, and file cabinets. As you enter your room-to-be, get a "feel" for the room. Is it hospitable? Gloomy?

☐ ☐ Count desks and chairs and tables—have you enough for each child? Do not start the term without a place for each child to sit, to work, to be.

Be careful! Student desks, chairs and tables come in many different sizes. Is your room's furniture appropriate for the age group? For example, if you will be teaching fifth grade, be sure you haven't been stuck with surplus second-graders' desks and kindergarten-sized chairs! No matter what grade you will teach, always keep a few larger desks and chairs on hand for heavy and/or taller students. If you're not sure, a little too large is better than a little too small. (Check the legs of the desks and chairs—the height of some can easily be adjusted with a Phillips-head screwdriver.) Arrange the desks/tables and chairs in any orderly pattern. You can rearrange them before school begins.

☐ ☐ Closets: Are there closets for supplies? A closet for your things? A closet for student coats and hats?

☐ ☐ Windows: Try the shades. Do they work? Try all the windows. Do they work? Are any windows broken? Are they in need of cleaning?

☐ ☐ Light: Turn off the lights—is there much natural light? Turn on the lights—how adequate is the lighting? (If the room is cold, fluorescent lights will be dimmer than usual, or they may not work at all. Try them again when the room is warmer.)

❏ ❏ Heating/cooling: Is there a thermostat or temperature sensor in the classroom? Does it work? (Open a window for a brief time to "kick" it on.)

❏ ❏ Odors: Does the room smell bad? If so, find out why.

❏ ❏ Safety: Are there any obvious unsafe items such as cracked/ broken glass, cracks in floor or walls, exposed insulation, wires that are bare or "pull-able," jutting nails, or clothing hooks at eye level of a student or teacher? Is there any loose, friable insulation on pipes or walls? If so, find out if the school is safe from asbestos hazards. Even if it contains no asbestos, friable insulation is not acceptable. Look up: Is the ceiling in good shape? Are there cracks or bulges? Some schools (especially those in the inner city) are more than 100 years old. You may be the first person in many years who has examined conditions in the classroom!

❏ ❏ Exits: Are there at least two classroom exits? (Older buildings might have only one exit.) Inspect the locks on the doors: Could you or your students accidentally get locked in? Locked out?

❏ ❏ Furniture: for you and for your students. File cabinets, desks, tables, chairs, cubbies, bookcases. Look them over. Hold your hand on each piece and gently rock it back and forth. Are any broken? (Are bookcases anchored to a wall? Students have been known to climb them as they would a ladder.)

❏ ❏ Audio-visual equipment: Is there any A/V equipment in the room? Does it work?

❏ ❏ School walk: Walk through the school. Locate the nearest exit for your classroom. Find way to lunchroom, gym, library, office, nurse.

❏ ❏ Outside: Look over the place for recess. Are there any potential trouble spots (trees, climbing structures, etc.)? Places to hide out of sight of the adult in charge? Where will students have recess on a rainy day?

❏ ❏ Request any needed maintenance or repair. (Do not wait until the week before school starts!)

❏ ❏ P.S. Do you have a place to park your car?

NOTES:

Instructional

Basic instructional preparation:

👍 ✋

- [ ] [ ] From the school secretary or principal, obtain a copy of the board of education, district, or school policy manual. You may not think it is relevant, but if there is an accident or a lawsuit, the court will look at any board, district, or school policy on the issue. Some schools have policies on a variety of matters that affect your job: book selection, corporal punishment, homework amounts and assignments, Christmas presents, and so forth. In the event of a question or problem, your ignorance of school policy will not save you. Read the policy manual. If you question or disagree with a policy, discuss it with the principal or lead teacher.
- [ ] [ ] Get other documents such as teacher/student schedules, attendance/absence procedures, bathroom/out-of-room guidelines, procedures for emergencies, unexpected school closings (inclement weather, for example), and school rules. Student and/or parent handbooks are also important to read through.
- [ ] [ ] Find out how many students will be in your class.
- [ ] [ ] Get a plan book, an attendance book, and a grade book. (Before you buy them, ask if the school provides them.) Even if your school administration does not check teachers' plan books, be sure to get one anyway, and use it.
- [ ] [ ] Obtain supplies, at least enough to see you through the first month or so. Essentials include chalk, chalkboard erasers, pencils, wastebasket, tape, stapler, and paper. Any other supplies you'll need?
- [ ] [ ] Bring home a copy of student textbooks so you may familiarize yourself with each.
- [ ] [ ] Find out what you are supposed to teach. Locate the curriculum for the school. Look it over. Think about how it applies to you and to your students. Using the curriculum and other resources, divide the year into units (big chunks of instruction). Do one subject at a time. (You can integrate instruction later.) For example, with fourth-grade math, divide the year into teaching units on basic operations, geometry, problem solving, measurement, fractions.

Managerial

Basic school/classroom procedures preparation:

☞ ✋

☐ ☐ Read school policies. Pay special attention to policies in areas
such as:

How to deal with student illness or injury.

What to do with students "at risk" because of health problems (e.g. hemophilia, AIDS, etc.). Review at-risk students
with a nurse, school psychologist, or counselor. Have a clear
idea of what course of action to take in the event of an emergency (such as the procedure for obtaining 911 assistance).

How to report suspected child abuse? To whom?

With whom should you share suspicions of student alcohol
and drug abuse?

What about prescription medicines sent in by parents?

☐ ☐ Write out a list of important school procedures. Specifically,
learn procedures that apply to field trips, emergencies, fire
drills, exits to use for lunch and dismissal, playground/
recess procedures and areas, and location of equipment. Tape
the list to the back of your plan book—use a highlighting
marker to mark crucial facts. Even if you learn them quickly,
leave it taped there. When you are absent, a substitute teacher
will need that information.

☐ ☐ Pick out a mentor or buddy teacher in your school. Is there
a "grade leader" (or any other experienced teacher) with whom
you can talk and ask questions as they arise? This will be a
very important advantage for you whether you are a beginning or veteran teacher.

☐ ☐ Locate records (permanent records) for your students. There
should be a folder for each child in your class. It will typically
contain health and academic records. Sometimes there are
"social" records as well. Have extra folders for temporary
folders for new students who arrive during the school year.

Skim the student records. Look for "special needs" students, including those with handicapping conditions, those
who are gifted/talented, students with a history of health or
behavior problems, students needing special arrangements

because of religion. Check for students whose parents have custody arrangements stipulating who may—and may not—pick up or otherwise remove a child from school.

☐ ☐ Write all student names in your attendance book. Enter "flags" for those special needs students and for those with custody, behavior, or health problems. To preserve confidentiality, make a mark in the column next to the name and be sure to provide an interpretive key for yourself (and for the substitute teacher).

☐ ☐ Count names. How many students will you have in all? Round your number up to the next five, just to be safe. For example, if 21 students are scheduled to be in your class, use 25 as your working number (to allow for the inevitable new students who enroll the first day of school). Even if you have a set list of students, round the number up. (I know this is mathematically impossible, but no teacher ever winds up with fewer students—somehow, every teacher gets more the first day of school!)

☐ ☐ Store all books and materials you will not be needing. Put them away—do not use valuable classroom shelf space for long-term storage.

☐ ☐ Compile "warm-up" activities you will use. Including age-appropriate activities for "ice breaking."

☐ ☐ Start thinking about the type of classroom climate you'd like to create. (Don't dismiss your ideas that you may see as "too idealistic"!) Review Abraham Maslow's (1970) "needs hierarchy." Low-level "deficit" needs (food, safety, acceptance, etc.) must be satisfied before higher-level "achievement" needs can be met.

☐ ☐ Write out several goals related to student health and well-being. For instance, how will you instill a feeling of safety for your students?

How about psychological safety—will you take a strong stand against rude behavior students may direct against each other? What basic understandings will you seek to establish?

How might you build classroom spirit? A sense of belonging? Your credibility as a teacher will spell the difference between success and failure—it is that vital. There are many ways that you can establish and strengthen your credibility in students' eyes. What might some of those ways be?

NOTES:

CHECKLIST II: PREPARATION—
2 WEEKS BEFORE TEACHING

Physical

☐ ☐ Seating and work areas: Arrange desks and furniture for the first day of school. Decide how you want them arranged based on your instructional style and plans. (If you're still not sure, arrange them in rectangular cluster groups of four to six desks.)

☐ ☐ Figure out "lines-of-sight" in your room in the following way: Stand near your desk. Walk to the chalkboard. Walk to the windows, then to the exit doorway. At each point, will you be able to see each student without obstruction? Conversely, will each student be able to see you?

☐ ☐ Traffic lanes: Picture students moving in the room. Will they move smoothly? Are there bottleneck points where students will bump into one another?

☐ ☐ Follow up on requests for repair or replacement of equipment.

☐ ☐ Check out recess equipment: What equipment will students use during recess? Where is equipment stored?

☐ ☐ Is some wall or bulletin board space vacant, ready for displaying your students' best works?

☐ ☐ Double-check: Any potentially dangerous conditions existing?

☐ ☐ Emergency procedures: Are they clear? Are they written down?

☐ ☐ Decorate. Make the room cheery and inviting. Bare or shabby bulletin boards are a desolate sight! Because you do not yet have student work to display, it is better to hang objects and pictures that relate to work you will be covering first, and store-bought decorations, than to have bare bulletin boards and walls.

Instructional

☐ ☐ Prepare materials for the first day such as name tags, cards, or headbands made of strips of heavy paper (for kindergarten through grade 2).

❐ ❐ Look through your portfolio or file folders. What can you use for your classroom? Find those wonderful lesson plans/unit plans you wrote for student teaching and include them in your teaching plan for this school year.

❐ ❐ Make copies of your class roster. List each student's name on the left in alphabetical order. Duplicate the list. You can use a copy to keep track of assignments, trip money, permission slips, and just about anything else. If you have access to a computer, placing the student list on it will save an enormous amount of time in doing these tasks.

Review your instructional expectations and make critical decisions:

❐ ❐ Participation: How will students be expected to participate?

❐ ❐ Solo and cooperative learning: Use "thirds" system—1/3 time work alone; 1/3 time work with partner; 1/3 time work as part of group?

❐ ❐ Getting help: When a student needs help to complete seatwork, what should he/she do to secure assistance? Ask a buddy? Ask the teacher? Display an individual "HELP, PLEASE" card or red flag?

❐ ❐ Will you expect students to raise hands before being recognized? Will you allow students to not raise hands? What should they do?

❐ ❐ Work procedures: What students must do when their work is completed. How is work to be submitted (When you ask? Automatically placed in their folder? Placed in your "in-basket"?).

❐ ❐ What will students who have finished do while others are still working? Work on an ongoing project? Go to a special interest/learning center? Post a chart of activities so you can point to it when a student says, "I'm done. What should I do now?"

❐ ❐ Late work: Will you accept it? If yes, how late? If not, why not? Under which circumstances will you accept it?

❐ ❐ Late finishers: If students have not finished when others have, what should they do? Finish it for homework? Finish it during recess? Finish it during any free time during the day?

❏   ❏   Homework: Will you assign homework each night? What will you do with homework the next day? Collect it? Have students check it? What if it's not done at all?

❏   ❏   Seatwork: (work students do at their desks, typically, alone). Seatwork usually consists of work assigned after a lesson, practicing a newly learned skill. Sometimes it involves drill. Seatwork must be done in a quiet area. Do not plan instruction or high activity when students are doing seatwork.

❏   ❏   Evaluation: How often will you give tests? What other evaluation techniques will you use? Conferencing? Performance tests? Projects? Authentic assessments?

Managerial
Decision time. Decide on:

👍 ✋

❏   ❏   Classroom jobs: Which jobs? How will you parcel them out? Who will do them? At what time or period during the day?

❏   ❏   Student supplies: How will students get supplies? Individually? By group?

❏   ❏   Absences: What is the school policy on absence? Are notes required?

❏   ❏   Lateness: What is the school policy? What will you expect them to do on entering late? Catch up? Work with a buddy? Jump right in?

❏   ❏   School procedures (playground, recess, assemblies). Write these down. What will your role and your class's role be in these events?

❏   ❏   Record keeping (report cards, grade book, progress reports, ways of communicating results to students and parents).

School movement:

❏   ❏   Where will you meet your students each day? (Will they come to the room, or will you go to meet them?)

❏   ❏   Lunch: Where will they eat?

❏   ❏   Recess: Where does this occur? What about when the weather is inclement?

❏   ❏ Special periods: Where and when will their "specials" (music, art, etc.) meet?

Classroom movement:
Individual student movement in and out of classroom:

❏   ❏ Leaving the classroom individually: Does the school require a hall pass? A sign-out book?

❏   ❏ Bathroom: How will students get to the rest room? Ask your permission each time? Just leave quietly? Take a partner? Sign out?

Group movement in and out of classroom:

❏   ❏ Line up? If so, by what criteria? By height? By "boys in one line, girls in another?" Assigned spots in line, or stand where you want?

❏   ❏ Procedures in preparing for lunch, special periods, activities, fire drill, going home, recess.

❏   ❏ Procedures for students to enter the room at start of day, after activity or recess, after lunch, fire drill.

❏   ❏ After school: What are dismissal routines?

Movement within classroom:

❏   ❏ Routines for sharpening pencils? Wastebasket? Learning center? Working in cooperative groups?

Student jobs:

❏   ❏ Jobs: watering plants, cleaning spaces, office monitor, supplies distributor/collector, snack, calendar.

Student seating and work areas:

❏   ❏ Seating: Once they enter the classroom, how will students know where to sit?
Will you assign seats? May they choose seats freely?

NOTES:

CHECKLIST III: FIRST-DAY PREPARATION

If you have been thorough in covering tasks in Sections I and II (above), this last section should be pleasant, if not easy. This section is mostly physical and managerial; you'll need to fill in the instructional details for your first day, such as content (what lesson you'll teach) and specifics that apply only to your school and teaching situation.

□ □ Print your name on the board: "Ms. Brooks." Identify the class: "Class 2-1." Use your best printing—children will model it.

□ □ Practice entering the classroom. If there is disorder upon entry, have students practice entering again: First line up the class to exit, then give a signal to exit: "Stop at first bulletin board in the hall. About face." Have students reenter the classroom.

□ □ Orient students to classroom, teacher, teacher's name, and one another. Will you have the students identify themselves?

□ □ Discuss expectations—theirs, yours, and both of yours together. Be clear on nonnegotiables.

□ □ Continue orientation. Where do students hang coats/clothing? Store their personal books and book bags? Lunches? Snacks?

□ □ Discuss basic student jobs. Who does what? When do they do it? Where do they do it? How will they be selected for these jobs?

□ □ Personal space. Point out what each child's private space (desk or table) is. Point out what your private space is.

□ □ Limits. Clearly instill key, basic limits such as "Listen quietly while others speak." Be sure to clearly establish these limits now, so that you can have productive discussions of basic understandings later on! If you have chaos, interruption, and disorder during this very first discussion, stop. (It will not get better the second day; it will only get worse.) Start over, clearly restating the limits. If you must, start over again. Hard work and persistence on your part now will pay off for the rest of the school year.

❏   ❏   Once key limits are clear, lead a brief "practice discussion,"
         perhaps an extension of the earlier "listen while others speak."
         For example, "How we are like a family = sharing . . . con-
         sideration for others."

❏   ❏   Start to build a class ethic: For example, describe how we are
         like a family. Elicit from students what qualities we must
         exhibit to succeed—sharing, patience, consideration for oth-
         ers, helping others when you can, and so forth.

❏   ❏   Instruction: Teach a lesson the first morning, something that
         will help students get used to the new teacher and class.

❏   ❏   Winding down: Stop all activities 15 minutes before the bell/
         signal to leave the room. Clean up. Then have students prac-
         tice lining up for leaving the room. One practice run should
         suffice. Reteach this if it is not flawlessly done! Prepare stu-
         dents for the signal (bell, etc.) so that when the bell rings,
         students will line up flawlessly the very first time.

☺   Smile! You did it!

NOTES:

7

Reflective Practice for Better Teaching

THE ability to think about things that have occurred is one of the first cognitive abilities to appear in human infants. As we grow, we connect this ability to a concern for the future—we reflect upon what has happened and plan for what will happen. This reflection is an essential part of teaching (and a particularly essential component in classroom management). Indeed, teachers spend more time in evaluation-related activities than any other professionals, and they make more evaluations during their day than any others. Ironically, although teachers do a lot of evaluating, they may do little reflecting or thinking about their own work.

Reflection is thinking about what has taken place in the classroom in a systematic way. Reflection follows instruction, and it precedes preparation. Reflection is asking "What went well? What needs to change? How can it be better next time?" In schools, time for teacher reflection is rare. With so many pressures and stresses on teachers, the sheer busy-ness of the school day limits time to think about what has taken place. Nevertheless, reflection is fundamental to change. If we are to become the best teachers we can be, then we must gradually improve in our teaching skill and skill as a positive classroom manager.

Reflection drives our improvement. It guides us toward doing something better, more effectively. As an inner-city classroom teacher, I constantly asked myself, "How can I do a better job teaching these students?" "What technique worked?" "What idea did not work out at all?" These reflections opened me to trying something new or doing something differently.

Trying is the main word here. In order to be most helpful, reflection has to involve more than words; it must result in action. Some actual, physical, or concrete change must follow reflection, or else reflection is an exercise in wishes and fantasy.

The School Year Cycles of Reflection: Immediate and Comprehensive

Research (and common sense) tell us that self-evaluation is best when it is systematic. *Systematic* means that you do it regularly—after teaching a new lesson or at the end of a school day. (Most of us do this already in an informal—but often highly judgmental—way.) After instruction, we informally reflect on what went well. What did not work well? Over the course of the school year (and even during holiday periods), teachers should continuously reflect.

But what types of reflection? Effective teachers report that two types are necessary: immediate reflection and comprehensive reflection. Immediate is looking back over the day or week or month and asking ourselves what went well, what did not, and what we are going to do about it. Comprehensive reflection is more structured—it lists the physical, instructional, and managerial tasks and asks you to evaluate how well you're achieving each. Let's look first at how to do immediate reflections.

Immediate Reflection

There are four times during the school year when it is critically important for the teacher to do an immediate reflection:

1. At the end of the first day,
2. At the end of the first week,

3. The last week of December*, and

4. At the end of the school year.

(*the fourth month will vary if your school is on a year-round schedule.)
The following is an outline for immediate reflection:

AT END OF FIRST DAY:

What went well:

Proof:

What did not:

Proof:

Action (What I MUST change for tomorrow):

At the end of my first day of teaching, my immediate reflection
outline looked something like this:

AT END OF FIRST DAY:

What went well: *I established a safe climate in the class. The
students are looking forward to tomorrow. They like me. Whew!*

Proof: *During our group discussion all students participated,
and this cooperation seemed to carry over to recess. They also felt
comfortable with the new routines.*

What did not: *Math lesson bombed.*

Proof: *I rushed through the lesson. Many of the students did not
understand the concepts. They looked puzzled and had many questions I didn't have time to address.*

Action (What I MUST change for tomorrow): *Slow down. Cut down amount of content I want to cover. Allow more time for student questions.*

At the end of your very first week of teaching, do your second immediate reflection. Follow the same simple format:

AT END OF FIRST WEEK:

> **What went well:**
>
> **Proof:**
>
> **What did not:**
>
> **Proof:**
>
> **Action (What I MUST change for Monday):**

As with your first immediate reflection, select a few items for "what went well" but select only one item for "what did not." If you choose more than one, you will lose focus, you will become overwhelmed, and most likely, you will not make that important change. Reflection works the same way with classroom management issues: If routines are not smooth (students arguing over jobs, claims of unfairness, etc.), reflect. Take that reflection and follow it up with action.

Here's what my first week looked like:

AT END OF FIRST WEEK:

> **What went well:** *Most things are going well. Students seem to like me. Vocabulary words are challenging.*

Proof: *Students are doing their homework. Classwork seems to be done on time. Ginny brought me part of her lunch after I said how I was "always hungry!"*

What did not: *Noisiness. Misbehavior.*

Proof: *Students fool around too much while I am off working with other reading groups.*

Action (What I MUST change for Monday): *Make sure they understand I am working with other groups and cannot share my attention during those times. Talk to them about the importance of quiet during reading group time.*

At the end of my first week teaching, my immediate reflection told me that on the whole things were going well, but there were trouble spots starting to appear. In fact, this "Action" that I took did not solve the problem as well as I had hoped. "Talking to them" was important, but it took a later reflection (and input from a valued colleague) to really get a handle on the disruption during reading group time.

Here is the format (same as before!) for the third immediate reflection:

AT END OF DECEMBER:

What went well:

Proof:

What did not:

Proof:

Action (What I MUST change for the new year):

By Christmas break I was exhausted. The "What did not" work was still my reading groups: No matter how much I talked to them and got steamed, it seemed to do no good. I asked my next-door teacher to come in and observe. He graciously gave up two of his free preparation periods to do so. We sat in the teacher's room afterward and he helped me plan my Action for January: It was not too late for a fresh start.

The proof was (to him) obvious: My students who were most disruptive were those who were finished early. They had nothing to do, so they started quietly fooling around, then yelling, then physically pushing each other to the point where I had to intervene.

The action I took was to assign work that was (a) sufficiently challenging—no easy baby work in reading, and work that (b) was sufficiently lengthy so that they would not be done in 5 minutes. It had to be meaningful and complex. In addition, they had to have something concrete to do—on their own—once they finished their reading group work.

On the following pages I provide four immediate reflection worksheets. Use each worksheet to focus your reflections at each of the four immediate reflection points (at the end of the first day, the first week, December, and the school year). Remember: If your circumstances are particularly difficult (as mine became), get help with your reflections. Locate a colleague, or a nonjudgmental administrator with teaching experience, and sit and review your reflections. Brainstorm to come up with an action plan. Redraw your earlier action plan, if necessary. Work short term—look toward tomorrow, and come up with action for tomorrow. Work on only one problem—your biggest one. Don't allow yourself to be overwhelmed. Get yourself through one day before you start planning for a week or a month at a time, but do not ignore problems you are experiencing. They won't go away on their own!

First Immediate Reflection: AT END OF FIRST DAY:

What went well:

Proof:

What did not:

Proof:

Action (What I MUST change for TOMORROW):

Second Immediate Reflection: AT END OF FIRST WEEK:

What went well:

Proof:

What did not:

Proof:

Action (What I MUST change for MONDAY):

Third Immediate Reflection: AT END OF DECEMBER:

What went well:

Proof:

What did not:

Proof:

Action (What I MUST change for the NEW YEAR):

Fourth Immediate Reflection: AT END OF THE
SCHOOL YEAR:

What went well:

Proof:

What did not:

Proof:

Action (What I MUST change for THE FIRST DAY
OF SCHOOL):

Comprehensive Reflection

In addition to the times for immediate reflection, there are times when a more comprehensive reflection is called for. Whereas immediate reflection looks within ("How did I do today?"), comprehensive reflection asks you to look at each dimension of positive classroom management (physical, instructional, and managerial) and reflect: "How well am I addressing practices within each dimension?"

Drawn from the strategies and skills for positive classroom management discussed in Parts I and II, I have created the following comprehensive reflection checklists. First is a general prosocial checklist. Following that are physical, instructional, and managerial checklists.

I suggest that teachers carry out a comprehensive reflection once or twice during the year, perhaps once shortly after the start of school, and again near the end of the school year.

At each time, review each checklist by yourself, or have a mentor or trusted colleague go over it with you. Refer back to Parts I or II to refresh your memory. Determine which points need attention. Pick one or two from your "sorta" or "not yet" list, and come up with an action you will take in each case. Write out your plan of action. Bring it to work with you—place it on your teacher's desk. Tape it there and refer to it during the day. Always get your mentor/buddy teacher in on your plan.

	okay ☺	sorta ☺	not yet ☹
General Prosocial Checklist			
1. Have I made clear the basic understandings?	☐	☐	☐
2. Are limits clear?	☐	☐	☐
3. Are courtesies being practiced?	☐	☐	☐
4. Do I emphasize cooperation over competition?	☐	☐	☐
5. Is it clear that respect is not negotiable?	☐	☐	☐
6. Is achievement (teacher, student, others) valued?	☐	☐	☐
7. Are all students included?	☐	☐	☐
8. Do I emphasize safety?	☐	☐	☐

	okay ☺	*sorta* ☹	*not yet* ☹
Physical Prosocial Checklist			
1. Are the "nuts 'n' bolts" in place?	❏	❏	❏
2. Is the physical environment working well?	❏	❏	❏
3. Does my classroom feel like a safe and pleasant place to be?	❏	❏	❏

Instructional Prosocial Checklist

As I teach:

1. Do I communicate instructional expectations?	❏	❏	❏
2. Do I convey enthusiasm?	❏	❏	❏
3. Are students kept accountable for their work?	❏	❏	❏
4. Am I aware what happens outside my immediate focus?	❏	❏	❏
5. Are my students successful?	❏	❏	❏

Use of strategies:

1. Do I teach at the right level of difficulty? Easy? Hard?	❏	❏	❏
2. Do I break instruction into smaller learnings?	❏	❏	❏
3. Do I use patterning or association in each lesson?	❏	❏	❏
4. Is student work monitored?	❏	❏	❏
5. Is adequate time provided for student work?	❏	❏	❏
6. Does my teaching encourage cooperation?	❏	❏	❏
7. Do I have a sense of students' nonacademic strengths?	❏	❏	❏
8. Are students overly dependent on my directions?	❏	❏	❏
9. Are students interested in their work?	❏	❏	❏
10. a. Do I give helpful feedback to students?	❏	❏	❏
b. Is my feedback immediate and detailed?	❏	❏	❏

	okay ☺	sorta ☺	not yet ☹
11. a. Do I ask good questions?	☐	☐	☐
b. Do I respond well to student questions?	☐	☐	☐
12. a. Is my instruction flow smooth?	☐	☐	☐
b. Is the pace about right?	☐	☐	☐

Managerial Prosocial Checklist

When faced with misbehavior, do I:

1. Keep things moving?	☐	☐	☐
2. Identify and deal with it easily?	☐	☐	☐
3. Maintain dignity—mine and the students'?	☐	☐	☐
4. Deal with misbehavior as quickly as possible?	☐	☐	☐

When interventions are necessary, do I use:

1. Noninterventions?	☐	☐	☐
2. Signal interventions?	☐	☐	☐
3. Physical closeness interventions?	☐	☐	☐
4. Humor interventions?	☐	☐	☐
5. Private verbal interventions?	☐	☐	☐

Do I avoid:

1. Harsh, public interventions?	☐	☐	☐
2. Punitive physical interventions?	☐	☐	☐

When faced with particularly serious problem behaviors, which of these strategies have I used?

1. Talking to student, use of "I-messages"	☐	☐	☐
2. Loss of classroom privileges	☐	☐	☐
3. Exclusion from class	☐	☐	☐
4. Student reflective activities	☐	☐	☐
5. Prosocial detention	☐	☐	☐
6. Parental involvement	☐	☐	☐
7. Daily (or weekly) report card	☐	☐	☐
8. Self-instruction strategies	☐	☐	☐
9. Contracts	☐	☐	☐
10. Involving the principal and/or other professionals	☐	☐	☐

	okay ☺	sorta ☺	not yet ☹

*If faced with a potentially harmful situation,
did I (or will I):*
1. Restrain myself from striking a student? ❒ ❒ ❒
2. Seek help? ❒ ❒ ❒
3. Avoid rash action, waiting for calm
   before proceeding? ❒ ❒ ❒

NOTES:

Conclusion

Being Your Own Best Teacher

I would not want anyone to have seen me in action in my first year of teaching. (Thank God no such videotape exists!) No, I didn't hurt any kids; I did no damage, and I worked really hard at teaching, but I was far from being the best teacher I could be. My classroom management skills relied heavily on personality—I wanted the students to like me. After all, I liked them, didn't I? So it was a real shock when students—whom I liked—started acting up, acting out, and making my life as a new and inexperienced teacher miserable. I took misbehavior personally. In retrospect, it was a learning experience. In fact, I believe that the first few years of teaching are when a teacher truly learns how to teach. It doesn't happen in college, nor does it come in student teaching. These are important, but only in setting a foundation. We learn to teach by teaching. We learn to manage classrooms by doing, not by talking about doing.

As I said earlier, my Aunt Flora was my role model and inspired me to want to become a teacher. After my first two years of teaching, I needed more than inspiration to make it work. I desperately needed concrete feedback from my colleagues. I'd invite them—beg them— to come into my room during their free period and observe me. Why was I having trouble managing the class? What could they suggest

101

to help me? They not only gave me feedback, they invited me into their rooms. I saw—and then imitated—strategies they shared and activities that worked with these same tough, inner-city children I taught.

By my third and fourth years of teaching, I can modestly say I was much better. By my fifth year I was awarded tenure, and my evaluations were excellent, but my significant improvement was when I began teaching students prosocial behavior. Our reading scores were up, but I became more skilled at teaching respectful behavior. I remember a tough classroom of inner-city sixth-graders (who had spent years joyously disobeying lists of rules). While I still had my "attractive power" (which all new teachers have during the first week or so of school), I created and communicated a clear direction of respect in our classroom. I explained that I expected them to respect other people. I expected them to also respect themselves. These were nonnegotiable. Furthermore, I devoted a great deal of class time discussing what the limits of respect were (such as students not taking things from others' desks without permission). I drew from students what they thought the courtesies of respect were (such as having teachers not making you feel small if you didn't do well on a test or forgot your homework). We spent a lot of time articulating examples of respect the first 2 weeks of school.

For instance, a dialogue from my sixth-grade class:

"Mr. D, the problem with teachers is that they don't respect kids."

"Yeah. Teachers want respect, but they don't deserve it."

"Mike, how can a teacher deserve respect?"

"By acting nice to students, and acting human."

"Matt, how could I act like I respect students?"

"Easy, Mr. D. By being nice, and not accusing us all the time of doing things we didn't do. Like Mr. Loftin in fifth grade. Nothing we ever did was right. He blamed me for everything—taking his pencils, breaking his stapler—everything."

"He had favorites, too."

"So it sounds like respect means caring about people's feelings."

"Yeah. If a teacher acts respectful, he'll get respected."

"Let me tell you a real incident: Once I saw a pencil fall on the floor and the student who picked it up—I'll call him 'Jack'—

said it was his. When Ann asked for it, he refused. He said
'finders-keepers, man. Finders keepers.' "
"Maybe Jack didn't know whose it was."
"But if Ann said it was hers, what should Jack have done?"
"He should ask another person, because maybe she's lying."
"He could do that. But remember respect? What's the respectful
thing for Jack to do? Sara?"

The key was that in addition to talking about respect, we practiced it as well. I led students in practicing how to work together in
cooperative groups, how to gather for lunch, how to borrow a pencil
from another, and how to ask a question in class. We spent a lot of
time going over basics of prosocial behavior.

With the basic understanding of respect for self and others as a
common ground, students will become more conscientious and less
focused on "getting away with" things. They become more prosocial as
they are able to generalize respect to other situations, situations for which
no explicit rules exist. They will not need a "NO LITTERING" sign in
any rest area or classroom they are in because they have internalized
respect for the environment and can carry it outside the boundary of
our classroom. When I took my sixth-grade class out of school on field
trips, they would receive compliments on their courtesy and good behavior. Yes, before the trip we talked—about where we would go, what
we'd see and do, and what the expectations were for safety and behavior. I never had to threaten them or recite a litany of new rules for being
out in public before the trip, for if throwing trash on our classroom floor
was not appropriate (and it was not), neither was throwing trash on the
floor of the New York City subway car; neither was throwing trash on
the floor of the greenhouse at the Brooklyn Botanical Garden.

I expect that my now-adult students still use a wastebasket to
this very day.

And open doors for others.

And say "Thank you."

And. . . .

Who knows where our influence ends? One of my very first students (whom I'll call "Jose") engaged in annoying and antisocial behavior. Both students and teachers seemed to avoid him. His mother
tried hard, too, but Jose displayed quite troublesome behavior at

home as well. As part of the school's fledgling music program, I purchased black plastic "song flutes" so my fourth-grade students could learn scales and some simple tunes. Jose took to the song flutes instantly. His reading and math scores were way below grade level, but he seemed to pick up sight reading and the fingering instantly. I'd let him solo for the class on occasion.

Several years later, on a visit to New York City, I ran into Jose's mother. She greeted me warmly and told me that Jose had been selected to play first clarinet in New York City's "All-City Orchestra." I was thrilled to hear the news. Since that day, Jose's success serves to remind me that all children have much potential and, if given the direction, will be able to use it in a constructive, prosocial fashion.

In summary: Before you can hope to teach students anything, you have to first create a secure learning environment for them. This means that you must use your power wisely, and use it to manage the classroom positively—in ways that foster prosocial student behavior.

Positive classroom management starts with considering the physical, instructional, and managerial aspects of teaching. Within these, preparing and reflecting are the action words you'll need.

Even if you are among the most experienced of teachers, you must continue to find out about your students—look for their strengths. Capitalize on those strengths, giving each student a chance to shine. The basics are important, but you must also promote the value of achievements other than reading, writing, and arithmetic. When you speak, ask questions that will arouse curiosity. Ask questions that will allow students to be successful, even in the mere act of answering a question. Let your students teach you what they know. The little things you do will make a tremendous difference in student success, and successful students are the easiest subjects for classroom management!

Teaching is a tough job, but the rewards for a job well done are without equal in any profession. Through preparation, reflection, and a willingness to do, you will become both "your own best teacher" and the best teacher you can be! Start today.

Our society needs it desperately!

References

Armstrong, T. (1994). *Multiple intelligences in the classroom*. Alexandria, VA: Association for Supervision and Curriculum Development.

Balikci, A. (1970). *The Netsilik Eskimo*. Garden City, NY: Natural History Press.

Beck, A. J., & Bonczar, T. P. (1994). *State and federal prison population tops one million*. United States Department of Justice press release of October 27, 1994. Annapolis Junction, MD: Bureau of Justice Statistics Clearinghouse.

Bloom, B. S. (1980). The new direction in education research: Alterable variables. *Phi Delta Kappan, 61*, 382-385.

Bryan, J., & Walbek, N. (1970). Preaching and practicing generosity: Children's actions and reactions. *Child Development, 41*, 329-353.

Buka, S., & Earls, F. (1993). Early determinants of delinquency and violence. *Health Affairs, 12*(2), 46-64.

DiGiulio, R. (1978, April). The "guaranteed" behavior improvement plan. *Teacher, 95*(8), 22-26.

DiGiulio, R. (1994). *Successful Vermont teachers describe their classroom practices*. Unpublished manuscript, Johnson State College, Vermont.

105

Durkheim, E. (1961). *Moral education* (E. K. Wilson & H. Schnurer, Trans.). New York: Free Press. (Original work published 1925)

Eisenberg, N., & Mussen, P. (1989). *The roots of prosocial behavior in children*. Cambridge, UK: Cambridge University Press.

Elkind, D. (1987). *Miseducation: Preschoolers at risk*. New York: Knopf.

Gardner, H. (1983). *Frames of mind*. New York: Basic Books.

Hartshorne, H., & May, M. (1930). *Studies in deceit*. New York: Macmillan.

Hoffman, M. L. (1979). Development of moral thought, feeling, and behavior. *American Psychologist, 34,* 958-966.

Joubert, J. (1928). *Pensées and letters of Joseph Joubert*. (H. Collins, Trans. and Ed.). New York: Brentano's.

Kohn, A. (1993). Rewards versus learning: A response to Paul Chance. *Phi Delta Kappan, 73,* 783-787.

Maslow, A. (1970). *Motivation and personality*. New York: Harper & Row.

McLuhan, M., & Fiore, Q. (1967). *The medium is the massage*. New York: Bantam.

Mercy, J. A., Rosenberg, M. L., Powell, K. E., Broome, C. V., & Roper, W. L. (1993). Public health policy for preventing violence. *Health Affairs, 12*(2), 7-29.

Metropolitan Life Insurance Company. (1986). *The Metropolitan Life survey of former teachers in America*. New York: Author.

Metropolitan Life Insurance Company. (1993). *The Metropolitan Life survey of the American teacher 1993: Violence in America's public schools*. New York: Author.

Murray, W. (1994, July/August). Have we got a design for you! *Instructor,* 59-62.

National Institute of Mental Health. (1982). *Television and behavior: Ten years of scientific progress and implications for the eighties, Vol. 1*. (DHHS Publication No. ADM 82-1195). Washington, DC: U.S. Government Printing Office.

New Hampshire Board of Education. (1853). *Seventh annual report upon the common schools of New Hampshire*. Concord, NH: Butterfield & Hill.

Reimer, J., Paolitto, D. P., & Hersh, R. H. (1983). *Promoting moral growth*. New York: Longman.

Shweder, R. A., Turiel, E., & Much, N. C. (1981). The moral intuitions of the child. In J. H. Flavell and L. Ross (Eds.), *Social cognitive development* (pp. 288-305). Cambridge, UK: Cambridge University Press.

Slavin, R. (1990). *Cooperative learning.* Englewood Cliffs, NJ: Prentice Hall.

Slavin, R. (1994). *A practical guide to cooperative learning.* Boston: Allyn & Bacon.

Wang, M. C., Haertel, G. D., & Walberg, H. J. (1993/1994). What helps students learn? *Educational Leadership, 51*(4), 74-79.

Whitmire, R. (1994, January 11). Study finds early steps critical to halting violence. *Burlington (VT) Free Press,* p. 10A.

Wolfgang, C. H. (1995). *Solving discipline problems.* Boston: Allyn & Bacon.

Zuckerman, D., & Zuckerman, B. (1985). Television's impact on children. *Pediatrics, 75,* 233-240.

Suggested Readings

Armstrong, T. (1994). *Multiple intelligences in the classroom.* Alexandria, VA: Association for Supervision and Curriculum Development.

Brubacher, J., Case, C., & Reagan, T. (1994). *Becoming a reflective educator: How to build a culture of inquiry in the schools.* Thousand Oaks, CA: Corwin.

DeVries, R., & Zan, B. (1994). *Moral classrooms, moral children.* New York: Teachers College Press.

Durkheim, E. (1973). *Moral education.* New York: Free Press.

Eisenberg, N., & Mussen, P. (1989). *The roots of prosocial behavior in children.* Cambridge, UK: Cambridge University Press.

Elkind, D. (1987). *Miseducation: Preschoolers at risk.* New York: Knopf.

Gardner, H. (1983). *Frames of mind.* New York: Basic Books.

Ginott, H. G. (1972). *Teacher and child.* New York: Avon.

Harmin, M. (1994). *Inspiring active learning: A handbook for teachers.* Alexandria, VA: Association for Supervision and Curriculum Development.

Kohn, A. (1993). *Punished by rewards.* Boston: Houghton Mifflin.

Krishnamurti, J. (1953). *Education and the significance of life.* New York: Harper & Row.

Lickona, T. (1991). *Educating for character.* New York: Bantam.

Lightfoot, S. L. (1978). *Worlds apart: Relationships between families and schools.* New York: Basic Books.

Ryan, K., & McLean, G. (Eds.). (1987). *Character development in schools and beyond.* New York: Praeger.

Slavin, R. (1994). *A practical guide to cooperative learning.* Boston: Allyn & Bacon.

Smilovitz, R. (1995). *If not now, when? Education not schooling.* Kearney, NE: Morris.

Wolfgang, C. H. (1995). *Solving discipline problems.* Boston: Allyn & Bacon.

Zehm, S., & Kottler, J. (1993). *On being a teacher: The human dimension.* Newbury Park, CA: Corwin.

Index

Achievement, student:
    and classroom management, 5
    and teacher expectations, 40-41
    is valued, 28-29
Ambience, classroom, 38-39
Armstrong, T., 47, 105
Awareness, teacher, 41

Balikci, A., 14, 105
Basic understandings:
    a "starter list" of, 26-30
    and prosocial behavior, 20-21
    teaching, 22-33
    See also Courtesies; Limits
Beck, A., 15, 105
Behavior:
    supporting positive, 54, 56
    See also Misbehavior; Violent
        behavior
Blaming, futility of, 1-3
Bloom, B., 50, 105
Bonczar, T., 15, 105
Broome, C., 21n, 106

Bryan, J., 31, 105
Buka, S., 7, 105

Checklist:
    comprehensive reflection,
        97-100
    for preparing your classroom,
        73-86
    general prosocial, 97
    instructional prosocial, 98-99
    mangerial prosocial, 99-100
    physical prosocial, 98
Classroom management:
    approaches to, 12, 14-15
    compared to business
        management, 13
    importance of, 4-7
    negative, 11-13
    See also Positive classroom
        management
Comprehensive reflection, 88, 97
    checklists for, 97-100
Consequences, prosocial, 16-17

in response to problem
behaviors, 62-68
Contracting, 49, 65
Cooperation, 27-28
Cooperative learning, 46-47
Corporal punishment, 61-62, 68
Corrective measures, 56-68
Courtesies, 23-33, 102
Crime and criminality, 15-16

Detention, prosocial, 64
DiGiulio, R., 4, 56, 105
Discipline. *See* Corrective
measures; Gallup Polls
Discussion, classroom, 26-30
Durkheim, E., 22, 106

Earls, F., 7, 105
Eisenberg, N., 17, 106
Elkind, D., 51, 106
Empathy in children, 18
Empowerment of students, 48-49
Enthusiasm, teacher, 41
Escalante, J., 40-41
Evaluation, 50-51
of student work, 47
self. *See* Reflection
Exclusion from class, 63
Expectations, instructional, 40-41

Fighting, reacting to, 66
Fiore, Q., 6, 106
Flow of instruction, 51-52

Gallup Polls, and discipline, 4
Gardner, H., 28, 47, 106
General Prosocial checklist, 97

Haertel, G., 5, 107
Hartshorne, H., 32, 106
Head Start, and prosocial behavior, 7
Hersh, R., 17, 106
Hoffman, M., 18, 106
Humor interventions, 58-60

"I-messages," using, 62-63
Immediate reflection, 87-92
worksheets for, 93-96
Inclusion, 29-30
Instructional dimension, 40-53
checklists, 76, 80-82
prosocial checklist, 98-99
12 useful strategies in, 44-53
Interventions. *See* Teacher
interventions

Joubert, J., 47, 106
Justice:
in children's thinking, 17-18
sense of distorted by rules,
19-20

Kohn, A., 32, 106

Legal system, a poor model for
classroom management,
15-21
Limits, 19, 23-33, 63-64, 82-83, 102

Managerial dimension, 54-68
checklists, 77-78, 82-83
prosocial checklist, 99-100
useful strategies in, 62-66
Maslow, A., 78, 106
May, M., 32, 106
McLuhan, M., 6, 106
Mercy, J., 21n, 106
Metropolitan Life Insurance
Company, 2, 5, 7, 106
Misbehavior:
correcting, 54, 56-68
four beliefs in response to,
57-58
preventing, 54-55
Moral behavior, 22-23, 32
See also Prosocial behavior
Morality, in children's thinking,
17-18
Motivation. *See* Students' interest
in learning

Much, N., 17, 106
Multiple Intelligences in the
    Classroom, 47
Multiple intelligences theory, 47
Murray, W., 39, 106
Mussen, P., 17, 106

National Institute of Mental
    Health, 6, 106
Netsilik Eskimos, 14, 16, 19, 29
New Hampshire Board of
    Education, 1, 106
Nonverbal interventions, 58

Pacing of instruction, 51-52
Paolitto, D., 17, 106
Parents:
    and prosocial behavior, 31
    as objects of blame, 1-2
    involving, 64
Patterning and association, 45
Phi Delta Kappan, 4
Physical dimension:
    basic considerations of, 37-39
    checklists, 73-74, 80
    prosocial checklist, 98
Physical interventions, 61-62
Positive classroom management:
    and student success, 42-44
    basic understandings in, 22-33
    corrective measures in, 56-68
    definition of, 11
    moving past rules and
        reactions and toward, 11-21
    preparing the classroom for,
        71-86
    preventive measures in, 55
    reflective practice in, 87-100
    supportive measures in, 56
    the instructional dimension of,
        40-53
    the managerial dimension of,
        53-66
    the physical dimension of, 37-39
    See also Classroom
        management; Prosocial
        behavior

Powell, K., 21n, 106
Power, teachers' use of, 3-4, 13
Preparation. See Teacher
    preparation
Preventive measures, 55
Principal, involving the, 66
Prison, United States population
    in, 15
Privileges, loss of classroom, 63
Project Head Start. See Head Start
Prosocial behavior, 6-7, 15-21
    and classroom management, 12
    and the instructional
        dimension, 40-53
    and the managerial dimension,
        53-66
    and the physical dimension,
        38-39
    teachers' modeling of, 31, 33
    teaching of, 22-33
    See also Misbehavior
Punishment:
    effects on prosocial behavior,
        15-17
    in classroom management, 12

Questioning, by teacher, 50-51, 104
Questions, types of, 50-52

Reflection, comprehensive, 88
    checklist, 97-100
Reflection, immediate, 87-96
    worksheets, 93-96
Reflective activities, 63
Reimer, J., 17, 106
Report cards, daily, 64-65
Respect, for others, 18, 102-103
    is nonnegotiable, 26-27
Rewards, 31-33
Roper, W., 21n, 106
Rosenberg, M., 21n, 106
Rules:
    alternatives to, 20-33
    problems created by, 15-20

Safety, students' feelings of, 30

Schweder, R. 17, 106-107
Self-instruction strategies, 65
Slavin, R., 27, 47, 107
Social skills, durability of, 7
Solving Discipline Problems, 67
Stress, effects of on teacher, 11-12
Student achievement. *See*
    Achievement
Students:
    accountability of, 41
    as objects of blame, 1-2
    responsible for own learning,
      48-49
Students' interest in learning, 49-50
Student success:
    teaching for, 42
    three axioms for, 42-44
    12 teaching strategies for, 44-53
Supportive measures, 56

Teacher, being your own best,
    101-104
Teacher beliefs, and student
    misconduct, 56-57
Teacher interventions:
    and misbehavior, 57-62
    and serious misbehavior, 62-68
    stepladder of four levels of, 57-62
Teacher preparation, 4
    early, 71-79
    for the first day, 85-86
    2 weeks before teaching, 80-84

Teachers:
    and classroom management,
      4-7
    as objects of blame, 1-2
    traits of excellent, 3-4
Teaching, 40-53
    improvement in, 101-104
    See also Instructional dimension
Television, effects of, 6-7
Threats of assault, reacting to, 66-67
Time, use of in instruction, 46
Turiel, E., 17, 106-107

Verbal interventions, 60-61
Violent behavior:
    dealing with, 66-68
    increase in, 21n
    predictors of, 7

Wait time, 46
Walbeck, N., 31, 105
Walberg, H., 5, 107
Wang, M., 5, 107
Whitmire, R., 7, 107
Wolfgang, C. H., 67, 107
Worksheets:
    for immediate reflection, 93-96

Zuckerman, B., 6, 107
Zuckerman, D., 6, 107

CORWIN
PRESS

The Corwin Press logo—a raven striding across an open book—represents the happy union of courage and learning. We are a professional-level publisher of books and journals for K-12 educators, and we are committed to creating and providing resources that embody these qualities. Corwin's motto is "Success for All Learners."